FIFA World Cup

WORLD FOOTBALL
FIFA WORLD CUP Football Records

Copiright 2021
© **World Football**
Edited by **Raffaele Cammarota**

All rights are reserved. No parts of this book may be reproduced or transmitted in any form or by any means, electronic or mechanical, including but not limited to photocopying and recording, for any purpose without the express written permission.

FIFA World Cup

The complete Almanac with all the matches, results, statistics, data of all the World Cups since 1930 to today

BEST FOOTBALL
Edited by **Raffaele Cammarota**

FIFA World Cup

INDEX

The FIFA World Cup..7

World Cup history 17

General Statistics and Records..................................81

Notes..92

FIFA World Cup

THE FIFA WORLD CUP

The **FIFA World Cup**, often simply called **World Cup**, is an international association football competition contested by the senior men's national teams of the members of the Fédération Internationale de Football Association (FIFA). The championship has been awarded every four years since the inaugural tournament in 1930, except in 1942 and 1946 when it was not held because of the Second World War.

The current format involves a qualification phase, which takes place over the preceding three years, to determine which teams qualify for the tournament phase. The 21 World Cup tournaments have been won by eight national teams. Brazil have won five times, and they are the only team to have played in every tournament. The other World Cup winners are Germany and Italy, with four titles each; Argentina, France, and inaugural winner Uruguay, with two titles each; England and Spain with one title each.

The **World Cup** is the most prestigious association football tournament in the world, as well as the most widely viewed and followed single sporting event in the world. The cumulative viewership of all matches of the 2006 World Cup was estimated to be 26.29 billion with an estimated 715.1 million people watching the final match, a ninth of the entire population of the planet.

17 countries have hosted the World Cup. Brazil, France, Italy,

Germany, and Mexico have each hosted twice, while Uruguay, Switzerland, Sweden, Chile, England, Argentina, Spain, the United States, Japan and South Korea (jointly), South Africa, and Russia have each hosted once. Qatar will host the 2022 tournament, and 2026 will be jointly hosted by Canada, the United States, and Mexico, which will give Mexico the distinction of being the first country to host games in three World Cups.

SHORT HISTORY

The history of the World Cup began in 1928, when FIFA president Jules Rimet decided to establish a tournament for national teams. The first such competition took place in 1930 and consisted of a tournament with only the final stage in which the 13 nations accepted the invitation.

The competition has since evolved to include about 200 national teams affiliated to FIFA that compete in a long qualifying tournament held in the three years prior to the final stage.

From 1930 to 1970 the winners were awarded the Rimet Cup. Initially, this trophy was known as the Victory Cup or simply Victory, but in 1946 it was renamed with the name of FIFA President Jules Rimet, who had the idea to organize the first world championship. The trophy was designed by French sculptor Abel Lafleur and crafted from gold-plated sterling silver on a white/yellow marble base. In 1954 this base was replaced by a high base made of lapis lazuli. Overall it was 35 cm high and weighed 3.8 kilograms. It included a decagonal cup, supported by a winged figure representing Nike, the ancient Greek goddess of victory.

In 1970, Brazil won the tournament for the third time and, as required by the regulations, was allowed to enter into possession of the trophy. However, the cup was stolen in 1983 and never found again, suspecting it was probably fused by thieves.

It should be noted that this was not the only theft of the cup.

Before the start of the 1966 World Cup in England, the Cup, transported there by the Brazil holder for the tournament, was stolen by strangers and reappeared only after a few days, found (according to rumors) by a police dog along the way.

After 1970 a new trophy was established to replace the Rimet Cup, the **FIFA World Cup.** The experts of the World Federation, coming from seven nations, evaluated 53 different models; in the end the work of the Italian designer Silvio Gazzaniga was chosen.

The same sculptor described his creation as follows: "The lines are born from the base, going up in spirals, up to tighten the world. The figures represented are two athletes who rejoice in the moment of victory".

The new cup is 36,8 cm high, with a base diameter of 13 cm, forged in 18 carat gold, empty inside but still heavy 6142 g. The base contains two bands of malachite (a semi-precious stone) and in the part below the base are engraved on a gold plate the names and the year of the nationals who have imposed themselves in the league since 1974.

The original version of the trophy, owned by FIFA, has a commercial value of approximately 155,000 euros (variable depending on the gold market price, figure updated in July 2018)even if its possible sale at a collector's auction would lead to a far higher valuation, if not immeasurable given the inestimable value as a work of art.

The cup was manufactured by Gde Licensee Bertoni of Paderno Dugnano (Milan) and is the same company that also takes care of its restoration or the remaking of any damaged parts, in frequent cases in which the trophy suffers damage. Until 2006, in fact, the winners of the cup remained in possession until the next edition: at the time of retirement the trophy was replaced with a copy of the same size but made of gold metal and subsequently laminated in gold. Since 2006 FIFA has decided to change regulations: due to numerous dents that forced it to an expensive restoration work, the federation decided to grant the original only for the award ceremony and for the next two hours under close surveillance; Immediately after the original is collected and kept in Switzerland, at the headquarters of FIFA and the winning national team is awarded the gold laminated copy. Even these copies are produced by the Milanese company, but none of these can be made without prior permission from FIFA.

This trophy will never be awarded permanently to a nation, regardless of the number of victories achieved, however the work of Gazzaniga could be replaced if the gold plate placed under the base of the trophy (therefore not visible without raising the trophy itself) should there be no more space available to engrave the name of the winning national team. To postpone this event as far ahead as possible in time, after the 2014 World Cup the vertical alignment of the names of the world champions nations engraved on the plate was redesigned to fit future title holders. The old gold plate has been replaced by a new one, in which the list of world champions since 1974 has been reorganized in a spiral to accommodate as many names as possible of the winners of future editions of the tournament. At the moment we cannot determine with certainty when this space will also be finished, since it is impossible to know in advance the names (and their length) of the future winning nations of the World Cup.

Since September 2008, the winning national team has been given the opportunity to display the FIFA Champions Badge, with a stylized version of the World Cup and under the inscription FIFA WORLD

CHAMPIONS and the year in which the national team won the competition. The national team awarded with the aforementioned coat of arms will be able to show on their shirt the badge until the final whistle of the next edition of the World Cup.

TOURNAMENT FORMULA

Since 1938, the organizing state obtains automatic participation in the final stage, this even when to organize it are more nations jointly (as already happened for Japan and South Korea in the 2002 edition). This will also be the case for the 2026 edition, which for the first time in the history of the World Cup will be hosted by 3 Nations at the same time, namely Canada, USA and Mexico. In fact, in the submission of the joint nomination it was anticipated that all three host nations will automatically be qualified for the final stage.

The current final tournament has been used since 1998 and features 32 national teams competing over the course of a month in the host nation. There are two stages: the group stage followed by the knockout stage.

In the group stage, teams compete within eight groups of four teams each. Eight teams are seeded, including the hosts, with the other seeded teams selected using a formula based on the FIFA World Rankings and/or performances in recent World Cups, and drawn to separate groups. The other teams are assigned to different "pots", usually based on geographical criteria, and teams in each pot are drawn at random to the eight groups. Since 1998, constraints have been applied to the draw to ensure that no group contains more than two European teams or more than one team from any other confederation.

Each group plays a round-robin tournament, in which each team is scheduled for three matches against other teams in the same group. This means that a total of six matches are played within a group.

The last round of matches of each group is scheduled at the same time to preserve fairness among all four teams.

The top two teams from each group advance to the knockout stage. Points are used to rank the teams within a group. Since 1994, three points have been awarded for a win, one for a draw and none for a loss (before, winners received two points).

From the second edition (1934) before the final stage are held the qualifiers to narrow the field of the national teams that will play the cup. This preliminary phase is held in the six different areas chosen by FIFA (Africa, Asia, Central-North America and Caribbean, South America, Oceania, Europe), and is organized and supervised by the respective confederations. For each zone, the world body decides the number of places put up for grabs generally based on the strength of the participating teams (in consideration of the results obtained). The qualifying tournament begins three years before the final stage and lasts for more than two years. The development of this phase varies according to the confederation; usually one or two of the places to be allocated are decided by direct elimination matches involving nations from different areas, for example, the winner of the Oceania area played against the fifth of the single group of South America to qualify for the 2006 World Cup.

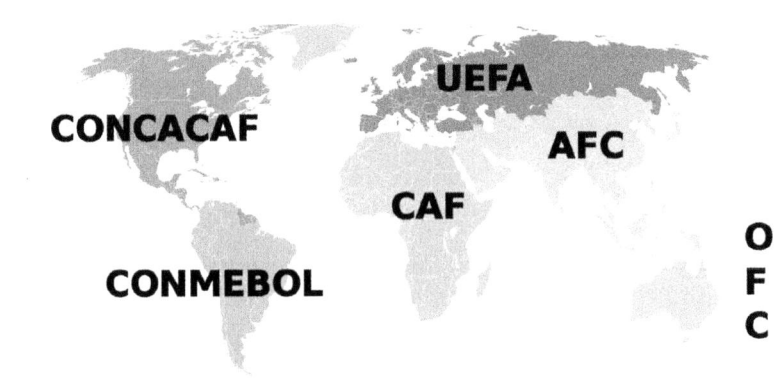

UEFA
CONCACAF
AFC
CAF
CONMEBOL
OFC

FIFA World Cup

WINNERS LIST

RIMET CUP

1930	URUGUAY
1934	ITALY
1938	ITALY
1950	URUGUAY
1954	WEST GERMANY
1958	BRAZIL
1962	BRAZIL
1966	ENGLAND
1970	BRAZIL

WORLD CUP

1974	WEST GERMANY
1978	ARGENTINA
1982	ITALY
1986	ARGENTINA
1990	WEST GERMANY
1994	BRAZIL
1998	FRANCE
2002	BRAZIL
2006	ITALY
2010	SPAIN
2014	GERMANY
2018	FRANCE
2022	

All data are updated at the 2018 World Cup in Russia

WORLD CHAMPIONS — CUPS WON

Brazil : 1958 - 1962 - 1970 - 1994 - 2002	5
Italy : 1934 - 1938 - 1982 - 2006	4
Germany: 1954 - 1974 - 1990 - 2014	4
Uruguay: 1930 - 1950	2
Argentina: 1978 - 1986	2
France : 1998 - 2018	2
England : 1966	1
Spain : 2010	1

World Cup history Top Scores

1) MIROSLAV KLOSE (Germany): 16 goals in 24 appearances
2) RONALDO (Brazil): 15 goals in 19 appearances
3) GERD MULLER (Germany): 14 goals in 13 appearances
4) JUST FONTAINE (France): 13 goals in 6 appearances
5) PELÉ (Brazil): 12 goals in 14 appearances
6) JURGEN KLINSMANN (Germany): 11 goals in 17 appearances
6) TEOFILO CUBILLAS (Peru): 11 goals in 13 appearances
6) SANDOR KOCSIS (Hungary): 11 goals in 5 appearances
9) GRZEGORZ SIDE (Poland): 10 goals in 20 appearances
9) THOMAS MULLER (Germany): 10 goals in 16 appearances
9) GARY LINEKER (England): 10 goals in 12 appearances
9) GABRIEL OMAR BATISTUTA (Argentina): 10 goals in 12 appearances
9) HELMUT RAHN (Germany): 10 goals in 10 appearances
14) PAOLO ROSSI (Italy): 9 goals in 14 appearances
14) ROBERTO BAGGIO (Italy): 9 goals in 16 appearances
14) CHRISTIAN VIERI (Italy): 9 goals in 9 appearances
14) UWE SEELER (Germany): 9 goals in 21 appearances
14) KARL-HEINZ RUMMENIGGE (Germany): 9 goals in 19 appearances
14) JAIRZINHO (Brazil): 9 goals in 16 appearances
14) DAVID VILLA (Spain): 9 goals in 12 appearances
14) VAVÁ (Brazil): 9 goals in 10 appearances
14) EUSEBIO (Portugal): 9 goals in 6 appearances

FIFA World Cup

Top Scorers every single World Cup

URUGUAY 1930 - STABLE (ARGENTINA) 8 GOALS
ITALY 1934 - NEJEDLY (CZECHOSLOVAKIA) 5 GOALS
FRANCE 1938 - LEONIDAS (BRAZIL) 7 GOALS
BRAZIL 1950 - ADEMIR (BRAZIL) 8 GOALS
SWITZERLAND 1954 - KOCSIS (HUNGARY) 11 GOALS
SWEDEN 1958 - FONTAINE (FRANCE) 13 GOALS
CHILE 1962 - ALBERT (HUNGARY), VAVÀ AND GARRINCHA (BRAZIL), SANCHEZ (CHILE), IVANOV (U.S.S.R.), JERKOVIC (YUGOSLAVIA) 4 GOALS
ENGLAND 1966 - EUSEBIO (PORTUGAL) 9 GOALS
MEXICO 1970 - MULLER (WEST GERMANY) 10 GOALS
WEST GERMANY 1974 - LATO (POLAND) 7 GOALS
ARGENTINA 1978 - KEMPES (ARGENTINA) 6 GOALS
SPAIN 1982 - ROSSI (ITALY) WITH 6 GOALS
MEXICO 1986 - LINEKER (ENGLAND) 6 GOALS
ITALY 1990 - SCHILLACI (ITALY) 6 GOALS
USA. 1994 - STOICKOV (BULGARIA) AND SALENKO (RUSSIA) 6 GOALS
FRANCE 1998 - SUKER (CROATIA) 6 GOALS
JAPAN AND SOUTH KOREA 2002 - RONALDO (BRAZIL) 8 GOALS
GERMANY 2006 - KLOSE (GERMANY) 5 GOALS
SOUTH AFRICA 2010 - MULLER (GERMANY), VILLA (SPAIN), SNEIJDER (NETHERLANDS) AND FORLAN (URUGUAY) 5 GOALS
BRAZIL 2014 - RODRIGUEZ (COLOMBIA) 6 GOALS
RUSSIA 2018 - HARRY KANE (ENGLAND) 6 GOALS
QATAR 2022 _____

FIFA World Cup

World Cup History

FIFA World Cup

1930 in Uruguay
Winner: URUGUAY

GROUP 1
FRANCE - MEXICO 4-1
ARGENTINA - FRANCE 1-0
CHILE - MEXICO 3-0
ARGENTINA - MEXICO 6-3
CHILE - FRANCE 1-0
ARGENTINA - CHILE 3-1
Qualified: **ARGENTINA**

GROUP 2
YUGOSLAVIA - BRAZIL 2-1
YUGOSLAVIA - BOLIVIA 4-0
BRAZIL - BOLIVIA 4-0
Qualified: **YUGOSLAVIA**

GROUP 3
ROMANIA - PERU 3-1
URUGUAY - PERU 1-0
URUGUAY - ROMANIA 4-0
Qualified: **URUGUAY**

GROUP 4
UNITED STATES - BELGIUM 3-0
UNITED STATES - PARAGUAY 3-0
PARAGUAY - BELGIUM 1-0
Qualified: **UNITED STATES**

SEMIFINALS
ARGENTINA - UNITED STATES 6-1
URUGUAY - YUGOSLAVIA 6-1

FINAL
30/07/1930 **URUGUAY - ARGENTINA 4-2**
12' Dorado (URU), 20' Peucelle (ARG), 38' Stabile (ARG), 58' Cea (URU), 68' Iriarte (URU) 89' Castro (URU)

FINAL RANKING

1° **URUGUAY**   2° Argentina   3° United States / Yugoslavia

WORLD CUP DATA

Edition I

Period from 13 to 30 July 1930

Organising country Uruguay

Host cities Montevideo

Teams participating 13

Total audience 434,500

Spectators per game 24.139

Matches played 18

Scorers 37

Goals scored 70

Goals per game 3,88

Penalties 3

Players participating 190

Players sent off 1

The youngest Carvalho Leita (Brazil) 18 years 65 days

Veteran Rafael Gutierrez (Mexico) 34 years and 149 days

Top scorer Guillermo Stabile (Argentina) with 8 goals

POSTER

STAMP

FIFA World Cup
1934 in Italy
Winner: **ITALY**

ROUND OF 16
ITALY - UNITED STATES 7-1
18 '29' and 64 'Schiavio (ITA), 20' Orsi (ITA), 57 'Donelli (USA),
63 'Ferrari (ITA), 69' Orsi (ITA), 90 'Meazza (ITA)
SWITZERLAND - NETHERLANDS 3-2
CZECHOSLOVAKIA - ROMANIA 2-1
HUNGARY - EGYPT 4-2
SPAIN - BRAZIL 3-1
GERMANY - BELGIUM 5-2
AUSTRIA - FRANCE 3-2 d.t.s.
SWEDEN - ARGENTINA 3-2
Qualified: ITALY - SWITZERLAND - CZECHOSLOVAKIA
HUNGARY - SPAIN - GERMANY - AUSTRIA - SWEDEN

QUARTER-FINALS
ITALY - SPAIN 1-1 d.t.s.
29' Regueiro (SPA), 44' Ferrari (ITA)
GERMANY - SWEDEN 2-1
AUSTRIA - HUNGARY 2-1
CZECHOSLOVAKIA - SWITZERLAND 3-2
ITALY - SPAIN (Repetition) 1-0 12' Meazza
Qualified: GERMANY - AUSTRIA - CZECHOSLOVAKIA - ITALY

SEMI-FINALS
ITALY - AUSTRIA 1-0
21' Guaita
CZECHOSLOVAKIA - GERMANY 3-1

FINAL 3° PLACE
GERMANY - AUSTRIA 3-2

FINAL
10/06/1934
ITALY - CZECHOSLOVAKIA 2-1 d.t.s.
71' Puc (TCH), 81' Orsi (ITA), 95' Schiavio (ITA)

ITALY: Combi, Monzeglio, Allemandi, Ferraris IV, Monti, Bertolini, Guaita, Meazza, Schiavio, Ferrari, Orsi
Head coach: Pozzo
CZECHOSLOVAKIA: Planicka, Zenisek, Ctyroki, Kostalek, Cambal, Krcil, Junek, Svoboda, Sobotka, Nejedly, Puc
Head coach: Petru
Referee: Eklind (Sweden) - Spectators: 45.000
Fascist Stadium Rome

FINAL RANKING
1° **ITALY**
2° **Czechoslovakia**
3° **Germany**
4° **Austria**

WORLD CUP DATA

Edition II
Period from 27 May to 10 June 1934
Organizing country Italy
Host cities Bologna, Florence, Genoa, Milan, Naples, Rome, Turin, Trieste
Teams participating 16
Total audience 395,000
Spectators per match 23.235
Matches played 17
Scorers 45
Goals scored 70
Goals per match 4,11
Penalties 4
Players participating 207
Players sent off 1
The youngest Roberto Iraneta (Argentina) 18 years and 65g
Veteran Thomas Florie (USA) 36 years and 262 g
Top scorer Edmund Conen (Germany), Oldrich Nejedly (Czechoslovakia) and Angelo Schiavio (Italy) with 4 goals

POSTER

STAMP

1938 in France
Winner: ITALY

ROUND OF 16
GERMANY - SWITZERLAND 1-1 d.t.s.
ITALY - NORWAY 2-1 d.t.s.
2' Ferraris II (ITA), 83' Brustad (NOR), 94' Piola (ITA)
CUBA - ROMANIA 3-3 d.t.s.
HUNGARY - NETHERLANDS INDIES 6-0
CZECHOSLOVAKIA - NETHERLANDS 3-0 d.t.s.
BRAZIL - POLAND 6-5 d.t.s.
SWEDEN - AUSTRIA 2-1 N.D.
NOT DISPUTED beacuse the renunciation of Austria
CUBA - ROMANIA (repetition) 2-1
GERMANY - SWITZERLAND (repetition) 2-4
Qualified: **ITALY - FRANCE - HUNGARY - BRAZIL - SWEDEN**
CZECHOSLOVAKIA - CUBA - SWITZERLAND

QUARTER-FINALS
ITALY - FRANCE 3-1
9' Colaussi (ITA), 10' Heisserer (FRA), 52' and 72' Piola (ITA)
BRAZIL - CZECHOSLOVAKIA 1-1 d.t.s.
HUNGARY - SWITZERLAND 2-0
SWEDEN - CUBA 8-0
BRAZIL - CZECHOSLOVAKIA (Repetition) 2-1

SEMIFINALS
ITALY - BRAZIL 2-1
55' Colaussi (ITA), 60' rig. Meazza (ITA), Romeu (BRA)
HUNGARY - SWEDEN 5-1

FINALE 3° PLACE
BRAZIL - SWEDEN 4-2

FINAL
19/06/1938
ITALY - HUNGARY 4-2 d.t.s.
6' Colaussi (ITA), 8' Titkos (HUN), 16' Piola (ITA), 35' Colaussi (ITA), 70' Sarosi (HUN), 82' Piola (ITA)

ITALIA: Olivieri; Foni, Rava, Serantoni, Andreolo, Locatelli, Biavati, Meazza, Piola, Ferrari, Colaussi - Coach: Pozzo
HUNGARY: Szabo; Polger, Biro, Szalay, Szucs, Lazar; Sas, Vincze, Sarosi, Szengeller, Titkos - Coach: Schaffer
Referee: Capdeville (France) - Spectators: 60.000
Stade Olympique de Colombes - Paris

FINAL RANKING
1° ITALY
2 Hungary
3 Brazil
4 Sweden

WORLD CUP DATA

Edition III
Period from 4 to 19 June 1938
Organising country France
Host cities Antibes, Bordeaux, Le Havre, Lille, Marseille, Paris, Reims, Strasbourg and Toulouse
Teams participating 15
Total spectators 483,000
Spectators per match (average) 26,833
Matches played 18
Scorers 40
Goals scored 84
Goals per game 4,66
Penalties 5
Players participating 211
Players sent off 4
The youngest Bertus Van den Harder (Netherlands) 18 years 42 days
The veteran Willem Anderiesen (Netherlands) 34 years and 190 days
Top scorer Leonidas (Brazil) with 8 goals

POSTER

STAMP

FIFA World Cup
1950 in Brasil
Winner: URUGUAY

GROUP 1
BRAZIL - MEXICO 4-0
YUGOSLAVIA - SWITZERLAND 3-0
BRAZIL - SWITZERLAND 2-2
YUGOSLAVIA - MEXICO 4-1
BRAZIL - YUGOSLAVIA 2-0
SWITZERLAND - MEXICO 2-1
Qualified: **BRAZIL**

GROUP 2
SPAIN - UNITED STATES 3-1
ENGLAND - CHILE 2-0
UNITED STATES - ENGLAND 1-0
SPAIN - CHILE 2-0
SPAIN - ENGLAND 1-0
CHILE - UNITED STATES 5-2
Qualified: **SPAIN**

GROUP 3
SWEDEN - ITALY 3-2
SWEDEN - PARAGUAY 2-2
ITALY - PARAGUAY 2-0
Qualified: **SWEDEN**
Retired: India

GROUP 4
URUGUAY - BOLIVIA 8-0
Qualified: **URUGUAY**
Retired: SCOTLAND and TURKEY

FINAL GROUP
SPAIN - URUGUAY 2-2
BRAZIL - SWEDEN 7-1
BRAZIL - SPAIN 6-1
URUGUAY - SWEDEN 3-2
SWEDEN - SPAIN 3-1

16/07/1950
BRAZIL - URUGUAY (Decisive match) 1-2
46' Friaça (BRA), 58' Schiaffino (URU), 61' Ghiggia (URU)

FINAL RANKING
1° URUGUAY
2° Brazil
3° Sweden
4° Spain

WORLD CUP DATA

Edition IV
Period from 24 June to 16 July 1950
Organizing country Brazil
Host cities Belo Horizonte, Curitiba, Porto Alegre, Recife, Rio de Janeiro and São Paulo
Final ranking 1 Uruguay, 2 Brazil, 3 Sweden, 4 Spain
Teams participating 13
Total audience 1,337,000
Spectators per game (average) 60.000
Matches played 22
Scorers 44
Goals scored 88
Goal to match 4
Penalties 4
Players participating 191
Players sent off 0
The youngest Carlos Ibàñez (Chile) 18 years and 224 days
The veteran Stanley Matthews (England) 35 years and 151 days
Top scorer Ademir I (Brazil) with 9 goals

POSTER

STAMP

FIFA World Cup
1954 in Switzerland
Winner: **WEST GERMANY**

GROUP 1
YUGOSLAVIA - FRANCE 1-0
BRAZIL - MEXICO 5-0
FRANCE - MEXICO 3-2
BRAZIL - YUGOSLAVIA 1-1 e.t.
Qualified: **BRAZIL - YUGOSLAVIA**

GROUP 2
HUNGARY - SOUTH KOREA 9-0
WEST GERMANY - TURKEY 4-1
TURKEY - SOUTH KOREA 7-0
HUNGARY - WEST GERMANY 8-3
WEST GERMANY - TURKEY (play-off) 7-2
Qualified: **HUNGARY - WEST GERMANY**

GROUP 3
URUGUAY - CZECHOSLOVAKIA 2-0
AUSTRIA - SCOTLAND 1-0
URUGUAY - SCOTLAND 7-0
AUSTRIA - CZECHOSLOVAKIA 5-0
Qualified: **URUGUAY - AUSTRIA**

GROUP 4
SWITZERLAND - ITALY 2-1
ENGLAND - BELGIUM 4-4 e.t.
ITALY - BELGIUM 4-1
ENGLAND - SWITZERLAND 2-0
SWITZERLAND - ITALY (playoff) 4-1
Qualified: **ENGLAND - SWITZERLAND**

QUARTER-FINALS
AUSTRIA - SWITZERLAND 7-5
URUGUAY - **ENGLAND** 4-2
HUNGARY 4-2 BRAZIL
WEST GERMANY - YUGOSLAVIA 2-0
Qualified: AUSTRIA - URUGUAY - HUNGARY
WEST GERMANY

SEMIFINALS
HUNGARY - URUGUAY 4-2 e.t.
WEST GERMANY - AUSTRIA 6-1

FINAL 3rd PLACE
AUSTRIA - URUGUAY 3-1

FINAL
04/07/1954
WEST GERMANY - HUNGARY 3-2
6' Puskas (HUN), 9' Czibor (HUN), 11' Morlock (FRG), 18' e 84' Rahn (FRG)

FINAL RANKING
1° WEST GERMANY
2° Hungary
3° Austria
4° Uruguay

WORLD CUP DATA

Edition V
Period from 16 June to 4 July 1954
Organising country Switzerland
Host cities Basel, Bern, Geneva, Lausanne, Lugano and Zurich
Final classification 1 West Germany 2 Hungary
Teams participating 16
Total spectators 943,000
Spectators per game (average) 36.269
Matches played 26
Scorers 59
Goals scored 140
Goals per game 5,38
Penalties 8
Players participating 224
Players sent off 3
The youngest Pas Coskun (Turkey) 19 years and 41 days
The veteran Stanley Matthews (England) 39 years and 141 days
Top scorer Sandor Kocsis (Hungary) with 11 goals

POSTER

LOGO

FIFA World Cup
1958 in Sweden
Winner: **BRASIL**

GROUP 1
WEST GERMANY - ARGENTINA 3-1
NORTHERN IRELAND - CZECHOSLOVAKIA 1-0
CZECHOSLOVAKIA - WEST GERMANY 2-2
ARGENTINA - NORTHERN IRELAND 3-1
CZECHOSLOVAKIA - ARGENTINA 6-1
WEST GERMANY - NORTHERN IRELAND 2-2
Qualified: WEST GERMANY - NORTHERN IRELAND

GROUP 2
YUGOSLAVIA - SCOTLAND 1-1
FRANCE - PARAGUAY 7-3
YUGOSLAVIA 3-2 FRANCE
PARAGUAY - SCOTLAND 3-2
YUGOSLAVIA-PARAGUAY 3-3
FRANCE - SCOTLAND 2-1
Qualified:
FRANCE - YUGOSLAVIA

GROUP 3
WALES - HUNGARY 1-1
SWEDEN - MEXICO 3-0
MEXICO - WALES 1-1
SWEDEN - HUNGARY 2-1
SWEDEN - WALES 0-0
HUNGARY 4-0 MEXICO
Qualified: SWEDEN - WALES

GROUP 4
ENGLAND - USSR 2-2
BRAZIL - AUSTRIA 3-0
BRAZIL - ENGLAND 0-0
USSR - AUSTRIA 2-0
BRAZIL - USSR 2-0
AUSTRIA 2-2 ENGLAND
Qualified: BRAZIL - USSR

QUARTER-FINALS
WEST GERMANY - YUGOSLAVIA 1-0
FRANCE - NORTHERN IRELAND 4-0
BRAZIL - WALES 1-0
SWEDEN - USSR 2-0

SEMIFINALS
SWEDEN - WEST GERMANY 3-1
BRAZIL - FRANCE 5-2

FINAL 3rd PLACE
FRANCE - WEST GERMANY 6-3

FINAL
29/06/1958

BRAZIL - SWEDEN 5-2
4' Liedholm (SWE), 9' e 32' Vavá (BRA), 55' e 90' Pelé (BRA),
68' Zagalo (BRA) 80' Simonsson (SWE)

FINAL RANKING
1° BRAZIL
2° Sweden
3° France
4° West Germany

WORLD CUP DATA

Edition VI
Period from 8 to 29 June 1958
Organising country Sweden
Host cities Boraas, Eskilstuna, Halmstad, Helsingborg, Gothenburg, Malmo, Norrköping, Örebro, Sandviken, Stockholm, Västeras and Uddevalla
Final Ranking Brazil 1, Sweden 2, France 3, West Germany 4
Teams participating 16
Total audience 868.000
Spectators per game (average) 24.800
Matches played 35
Scorers 60
Goals scored 126
Goal per match 3,6
Penalties 10
Players participating 247
Players sent off 3
The youngest Pelè (Brazil) 17 years 235 days
Veteran Ángel Labruna (Argentina) 39 years 260 days
Top scorer Just Fontaine (France) with 13 goals

POSTER

LOGO

FIFA World Cup
1962 in Chile
Winner: **BRASIL**

GROUP 1
URUGUAY - COLOMBA 2-1
USSR - YUGOSLAVIA 2-0
YUGOSLAVIA - URUGUAY 3-1
USSR - COLOMBA 4-4
USSR - URUGUAY 2-1
YUGOSLAVIA - COLOMBA 5-0
Qualified: USSR - YUGOSLAVIA

GROUP 2
CHILE - SWITZERLAND 3-1
ITALY - GERMANY O. 0-0
CHILE - ITALY 2-0
GERMANY O. - SWITZERLAND 2-1
GERMANY O. - CHILE 2-0
ITALY - SWITZERLAND 3-0
Qualified: WEST GERMANY - CHILE

GROUP 3
BRAZIL - MEXICO 2-0
CZECHOSLOVAKIA - SPAIN 1-0
BRAZIL - CZECHOSLOVAKIA 0-0
SPAIN - MEXICO 1-0
BRAZIL - SPAIN 2-1
MEXICO - CZECHOSLOVAKIA 3-1
Qualified: BRAZIL
CZECHOSLOVAKIA

GROUP 4
ARGENTINA 1-0 BULGARIA
HUNGARY - **ENGLAND** 2-1
ENGLAND - ARGENTINA 3-1
HUNGARY BULGARIA 6-1
HUNGARY - ARGENTINA 0-0
BULGARIA - **ENGLAND** 0-0
Qualified: HUNGARY
ENGLAND

QUARTER-FINALS
CHILE - USSR 2-1
BRAZIL - **ENGLAND** 3-1
CZECHOSLOVAKIA - HUNGARY 1-0
YUGOSLAVIA - WEST GERMANY 1-0

SEMIFINALS
CZECHOSLOVAKIA - YUGOSLAVIA 3-1
BRAZIL - CHILE 4-2

FINAL 3rd PLACE
CHILE - YUGOSLAVIA 1-0

FINAL
17/06/1962
BRAZIL - CZECHOSLOVAKIA 3-1
15' Masopust (TCH), 17' Amarildo (BRA), 69' Zito (BRA), 78' Vavá (BRA)

FINAL RANKING
1° **BRAZIL**
2° Czechoslovakia
3° Chile
4° Yugoslavia

WORLD CUP DATA

Edition VII
Period from 30 May to 17 June 1962
Organising country Chile
Host cities Arica, Rancagua, Santiago and Viña del Mar
Winner Brazil
Teams participating 16
Total audience 776.000
Spectators per game (average) 24.250
Matches played 32
Scorers 54
Goals scored 89
Goals per game 2,78
Penalties 9
Players participating 247
Players sent off 6
The youngest Gianni Rivera (Italy) 18 years and 286 days
The veteran Nilton Santos (Brazil) 37 years and 32 days
Top scorer Florian Albert (Hungary), Garrincha (Brazil), Valentin Ivanov (USSR), Drazen Jerkovic (Yugoslavia), Leonel Sànchez (Chile) and Vavà (Brazil) with 4 goals

POSTER

LOGO

FIFA World Cup
1966 in England
Winner: ENGLAND

GROUP 1
ENGLAND - URUGUAY 0-0
FRANCE - MEXICO 1-1
URUGUAY - FRANCE 2-1
ENGLAND - MEXICO 2-0
37' B. Charlton, 75'Hunt
MEXICO - URUGUAY 0-0
ENGLAND - FRANCE 2-0
38', 75' Hunt
Qualified: ENGLAND URUGUAY

GROUP 2
GERMANY O. - SWITZERLAND 5-0
ARGENTINA - SPAIN 2-1
SPAIN - SWITZERLAND 2-1
GERMANY O. - ARGENTINA 0-0
ARGENTINA - SWITZERLAND 2-0
GERMANY O. - SPAIN 2-1
Qualified: WEST GERMANY ARGENTINA

GROUP 3
BRAZIL - BULGARIA 2-0
PORTUGAL - HUNGARY 3-1
HUNGARY - BRAZIL 3-1
PORTUGAL - BULGARIA 3-0
PORTUGAL - BRAZIL 3-1
HUNGARY - BULGARIA 3-1
Qualified: PORTUGAL - HUNGARY

GROUP 4
USSR - NORTH KOREA 3-0
ITALY - CHILE 2-0
NORTH CHILE-KOREA 1-1
USSR - ITALY 1-0
NORTH KOREA - ITALY 1-0
USSR - CHILE 2-1
Qualified: USSR - NORTH KOREA

QUARTER FINALS
ENGLAND - ARGENTINA 1-0 78' Hurst
PORTUGAL - NORTH KOREA 5-3
USSR - HUNGARY 2-1
WEST GERMANY - URUGUAY 4-0

SEMIFINAL
WEST GERMANY - USSR 2-1
ENGLAND - PORTUGAL 2-1
30', 80' B. Charlton, Eusébio 82' (rig.)

FINAL 3rd PLACE
07/28/1966
PORTUGAL - USSR 2-1

FINAL
30/07/1966
ENGLAND - WEST GERMANY 4-2 e.t.
12' Haller (FRG), 18' 101' e 120' Hurst (ENG),
78' Peters (ENG), 90' Weber (FRG)
Referee: Gottfried Dienst (Swi) - **Spectators**: 96 924
Stadium: Wembley Stadium

FINAL RANKING
1° ENGLAND
2° West Germany
3° Portugal
4° USSR

WORLD CUP DATA

Edition VIII
Period from 11 to 30 July 1966
Organizing country England
Host cities Liverpool, London, Manchester, Middlesbrough, Sheffield and Sunderland
Final ranking
England 1 West Germany 2
Portugal 3 Soviet Union 4
Teams participating 16
Total audience 1.614.677
Spectators per game (average) 50.459
Matches played 32
Scorers 45
Goals scored 89
Goals per match 2,78
Penalties 8
Players participating 253
Players sent off 5
The youngest Tostao (Brazil) 19 years 171 days
Veteran Djalma Santos (Brazil) 37 years and 171 days
Top scorer Eusébio (Portugal) with 9 goals

POSTER

LOGO

FIFA World Cup

1970 in Mexico
Winner: **BRASIL**

GROUP 1
MEXICO - USSR 0-0
BELGIUM - EL SALVADOR 3-0
USSR - BELGIUM 4-1
MEXICO - EL SALVADOR 4-0
USSR - EL SALVADOR 2-0
MEXICO - BELGIUM 1-0
Qualified: USSR - MEXICO

GROUP 2
URUGUAY - ISRAEL 2-0
ITALY - SWEDEN 1-0
ITALY - URUGUAY 0-0
SWEDEN - ISRAEL 1-1
SWEDEN - URUGUAY 1-0
ITALY - ISRAEL 0-0
Qualified: ITALY - URUGUAY

GROUP 3
ENGLAND - ROMANIA 1-0
BRAZIL - CZECHOSLOVAKIA 4-1
ROMANIA - CZECHOSLOVAKIA 2-1
BRAZIL - **ENGLAND** 1-0
BRAZIL - ROMANIA 3-2
ENGLAND - CZECHOSLOVAKIA 1-0
Qualified: BRAZIL - ENGLAND

GROUP 4
PERU - BULGARIA 3-2
GERMANY OR - MOROCCO 2-1
PERU - MOROCCO 3-0
GERMANY O. - BULGARIA 5-2
GERMANY O. - PERU 3-2
BULGARIA - MOROCCO 1-1
Qualified: WEST GERMANY - PERU

QUARTER-FINALS
ITALY - MEXICO 4-1
WEST GERMANY - **ENGLAND** 3-2 e.t.
BRAZIL - PERU 4-2
URUGUAY - USSR 1-0 e.t.

SEMIFINALS
ITALY - WEST GERMANY 4-3 e.t.
7' Boninsegna (ITA), 90' Schnellinger (RFG), 95'e 110' Müller (RFG),
98' Burgnich (ITA), 103' Riva (ITA), 112' Rivera (ITA)
BRAZIL - URUGUAY 3-1

FINAL 3° PLACE
WEST GERMANY - URUGUAY 1-0

FINAL
21/06/1970 Estadio Azteca - Città del Messico
BRAZIL - ITALY 4-1
BRAZIL: Félix; Carlos Alberto, Piazza, Brito, Everaldo, Clodoaldo, Gérson, Rivelino, Jairzinho, Tostao, Pelé - Coach: Zagalo
ITALY: Albertosi, Burgnich, Cera, Bertini, Rosato, Facchetti, Domenghini, De Sisti, Mazzola, Boninsegna, Riva - All: Valcareggi
Goals: 18 'Pelé (BRA), 37' Boninsegna (ITA), 66 'Gérson (BRA), 71' Jairzinho (BRA), 87 'Carlos Alberto (BRA)
Referee: Glöckner (West Germany) - Spectators: 108,000

FINAL RANKING
1° **BRAZIL**
2° Italy
3° West Germany
4° Uruguay

WORLD CUP DATA

Edition IX
Period from 31 May to 21 June 1970
Organizing country Mexico
HOST CITIES Guadalajara, Leon, Mexico City, Puebla and Toluca
Final Ranking Brazil 1, Italy 2, West Germany 3, Uruguay 4
Teams participating 16
Total audience 1.673.975
Spectators per game (average) 52.312
Matches played 32
Scorers 54
Goals scored 95
Goals per game 2,96
Penalties 8
Players participating 267
Players sent off 5
The youngest Marco Antonio (Brazil) 19 years and 124 days
Veteran Jack Charlton (England) 37 years 196 days
Top scorer Gerhard Müller (West Germany) with 10 goals

LOGO

MASCOTTE

FIFA World Cup

1974 in West Germany
Winner: **WEST GERMANY**

FIRST STAGE IN GROUPS

GROUP 1
EAST GERMANY - AUSTRALIA 2-0
GERMANY O. - CHILE 1-0
GERMANY O. - AUSTRALIA 3-0
CHILE - EAST GERMANY 1-1
AUSTRALIA - CHILE 0-0
EAST GERMANY - GERMANY O. 1-0
Qualified: EAST GERMANY - WEST GERMANY

GROUP 2
BRAZIL - YUGOSLAVIA 0-0
SCOTLAND - ZAIRE 2-0
YUGOSLAVIA - ZAIRE 9-0
SCOTLAND - BRAZIL 0-0
BRAZIL - ZAIRE 3-0
YUGOSLAVIA - SCOTLAND 1-1
Qualified: YUGOSLAVIA - BRAZIL

GROUP 3
SWEDEN - BULGARIA 0-0
HOLLAND - URUGUAY 2-0
BULGARIA 1-1 URUGUAY
HOLLAND - SWEDEN 0-0
HOLLAND - BULGARIA 4-1
SWEDEN - URUGUAY 3-0
Qualified: NETHERLANDS - SWEDEN

GROUP 4
ITALY - HAITI 3-1
POLAND - ARGENTINA 3-2
ITALY - ARGENTINA 1-1
POLAND - HAITI 7-0
ITALY - POLAND 1-2
ARGENTINA - HAITI 4-1
Qualified: POLAND - ARGENTINA

SECOND STAGE IN GROUPS

GROUP A
BRAZIL - EAST GERMANY 1-0
HOLLAND - ARGENTINA 4-0
BRAZIL - ARGENTINA 2-1
HOLLAND - EAST GERMANY 2-0
ARGENTINA - EAST GERMANY 1-1
HOLLAND - BRAZIL 2-0

GROUP B
WEST GERMANY - YUGOSLAVIA 2-0
POLAND - SWEDEN 1-0
POLAND - YUGOSLAVIA 2-1
WEST GERMANY - SWEDEN 4-2
SWEDEN 2-1 YUGOSLAVIA
WEST GERMANY - POLAND 1-0
Access to the final: **HOLLAND - WEST GERMANY**

FINAL 3° PLACE
POLAND - BRAZIL 1-0

FINAL
WEST GERMANY - HOLLAND 2-1
2 ' pen. Neeskens (Hol), 25 ' pen. Breitner (Ger), 43 ' Müller (Ger)

FINAL RANKING
1° WEST GERMANY
2° Holland
3° Poland
4° Brazil

WORLD CUP DATA

Edition X
Period from 13 June to 7 July 1974
Organizing country West Germany
Host cities Hamburg, Berlin, Dortmund, Düsseldorf, Frankfurt am Main, Gelsenkirchen, Hanover, Munich and Stuttgart
Final Ranking West Germany 1, Holland 2, Poland 3, Brazil 4
Teams participating 16
Total spectators 1.774.022
Spectators per game (average) 46.685
Matches played 38
Scorers 48
Goals scored 97
Goals per game 2,55
Penalties 8
Players participating 267
Players sent off 5
The youngest Vladimir Petrovic (Yugoslavia) 18 years and 364 days
The veteran Tarcisio Burgnich (Italy) 35 years 59 days
Top scorer Grzegorz Lato (Poland) with 7 goals

LOGO

MASCOTTE

FIFA World Cup

1978 in Argentina
Winner: ARGENTINA

FIRST STAGE IN GROUPS

GROUP 1
ITALY - FRANCE 2-1
ARGENTINA - HUNGARY 2-1
ITALY - HUNGARY 3-1
ARGENTINA 2-1 FRANCE
ITALY - ARGENTINA 1-0
FRANCE - HUNGARY 3-1
Qualified: ITALY - ARGENTINA

GROUP 2
GERMANY O. - POLAND 0-0
POLAND - MEXICO 3-1
GERMANY O. - MEXICO 6-0
POLAND - TUNISIA 1-0
TUNISIA - GERMANY O. 0-0
POLAND - MEXICO 3-1
Qualified: POLAND - WEST GERMANY

GROUP 3
AUSTRIA 2-1 SPAIN
BRAZIL - SWEDEN 1-1
AUSTRIA - SWEDEN 1-0
BRAZIL - SPAIN 0-0
SPAIN - SWEDEN 1-0
BRAZIL - AUSTRIA 1-0
Qualified: AUSTRIA - BRAZIL

GROUP 4
PERU - SCOTLAND 3-1
HOLLAND - IRAN 3-0
SCOTLAND - IRAN 1-1
HOLLAND - PERU 0-0
PERU - IRAN 4-1
SCOTLAND 3-2 HOLLAND
Qualified: PERU - NETHERLANDS

SECOND STAGE IN GROUPS

GROUP A
WEST GERMANY - ITALY 0-0
HOLLAND - AUSTRIA 5-1
ITALY - AUSTRIA 1-0
WEST GERMANY - HOLLAND 2-2
HOLLAND - ITALY 2-1
AUSTRIA - WEST GERMANY 3-2

GROUP B
ARGENTINA - POLAND 2-0
BRAZIL - PERU 1-0
ARGENTINA - BRAZIL 0-0
POLAND - PERU 1-2
ARGENTINA - PERU 6-0
BRAZIL - POLAND 3-1
Access to the final: HOLLAND - ARGENTINA

FINAL 3° PLACE
BRAZIL - ITALY 2-1
38' Causio (ITA), 63' Nelinho (BRA), 70' Dirceu (BRA)

FINAL 25/06/1978
ARGENTINA - HOLLAND 3-1 e.t.
38' e 104' Kempes (ARG), 82' Nanninga (HOL),
114' Bertoni (ARG)

FINAL RANKING
1° ARGENTINA
2nd Holland
3rd Brazil
4th Italy

WORLD CUP DATA

Edition XI
Period 1 to 25 June 1978
Organizing country Argentina
Host cities Buenos Aires, Còrdoba, Mar del Plata, Mendoza and Rosario
Final ranking 1 Argentina, 2 Netherlands, 3 Brazil, 4 Italy
Teams participating 16
Total spectators 1,541,518
Spectators per game (average) 40.566
Matches played 38
Scorers 59
Goals scored 102
Goals per game 2,68
Penalties 14
Players participating 76
Players sent off 3
Youngest Andrzey Iwan (Poland) 19 years 206 days
Veteran Jan Jongbloed (Netherlands) 37 years 212 days
Top scorer Mario Kempes (Argentina) with 6 goals

LOGO

Argentina 78

MASCOTTE

FIFA World Cup

1982 in Spain
Winner: ITALY

FIRST STAGE IN GROUPS

GROUP 1
ITALY - POLAND 0-0
PERU - CAMEROON 0-0
ITALY - PERU 1-1
POLAND - CAMEROON 0-0
POLAND - PERU 5-1
ITALY - CAMEROON 1-1
Qualified: POLAND - ITALY

GROUP 2
GERMANY O. - ALGERIA 1-2
AUSTRIA - CHILE 1-0
WEST GERMANY - CHILE 4-1
AUSTRIA - ALGERIA 2-0
ALGERIA - CHILE 3-2
GERMANY O. - AUSTRIA 1-0
Qualified: WEST GERMANY - AUSTRIA

GROUP 3
BELGIUM - ARGENTINA 1-0
HUNGARY - EL SALVADOR 10-1
ARGENTINA - HUNGARY 4-1
BELGIUM - EL SALVADOR 1-0
BELGIUM - HUNGARY 1-1
ARGENTINA - EL SALVADOR 2-0
Qualified: BELGIUM - ARGENTINA

GROUP 4
ENGLAND - FRANCE 3-1
CZECHOSLOVAKIA - KUWAIT 1-1
ENGLAND - CZECHOSLOVAKIA 2-0
FRANCE - KUWAIT 4-1
FRANCE - CZECHOSLOVAKIA 1-1
ENGLAND - KUWAIT 1-0
Qualified: **ENGLAND** - FRANCE

FIFA World Cup

GROUP 5
SPAIN - HONDURAS 1-1
YUGOSLAVIA - IRELAND 0-0
SPAIN - YUGOSLAVIA 2-1
HONDURAS - YUGOSLAVIA 0-1
HONDURAS - NORTHERN IRELAND 1-1
SPAIN - NORTHERN IRELAND 0-1
Qualified: IRELAND N. - SPAIN

GROUP 6
BRAZIL - USSR 2-1
SCOTLAND - NEW ZEALAND 5-2
BRAZIL 4-1 SCOTLAND
USSR - NEW ZEALAND 3-0
USSR - SCOTLAND 2-2
BRAZIL - NEW ZEALAND 4-0
Qualified: BRAZIL - USSR

SECOND STAGE IN GROUPS

GROUP A
POLAND - BELGIUM 3-0
USSR - BELGIUM 1-0
USSR - POLAND 0-0
Qualified: **POLAND**

GROUP C
ITALY - ARGENTINA 2-1
BRAZIL - ARGENTINA 3-1
ITALY - BRAZIL 3-2
Qualified: **ITALY**

GROUP B
GERMANY W - **ENGLAND** 0-0
GERMANY W. - SPAIN 2-1
ENGLAND - SPAIN 0-0
Qualified: **West GERMANY**

GROUP D
FRANCE - AUSTRIA 1-0
IRELAND N - AUSTRIA 2-2
FRANCE - IRELAND N. 4-1
Qualified: **FRANCE**

SEMIFINALS
ITALY - POLAND 2-0
WEST GERMANY - FRANCE 3-3 (8-7 AD)
FINAL 3RD PLACE: POLAND 3-2 FRANCE

FINAL 11/07/1982 - **ITALY** - WEST GERMANY 3-1

Italy: Zoff; Gentile, Cabrini, Bergomi, Collovati, Scirea, Conti, Tardelli, Rossi, Oriali, Graziani - Coach: Bearzot
West Germany: Schumacher; Kaltz, Forster, Stielike, Briegel, Forster, Dremmler, Breitner, Rummenigge, Littbarski, Fischer - All.: Derwall
57 'Rossi (ITA), 69' Tardelli (ITA), 81 'Altobelli (ITA), 83' Breitner

FINAL RANKING
1° **ITALY**   2° **West Germany**   3° **Poland**   4° **France**

WORLD CUP DATA

Edition XII
Period from 13 June to 11 July 1982
Organising country Spain
Host cities Alicante, Barcelona, Bilbao, Elche, Gijon, La Coruña, Madrid, Malaga, Oviedo, Seville, Valencia, Valladoid, Vigo and Zaragoza
Final ranking Italy 1, West Germany 2, Poland 3, France 4
Teams participating 24
Total spectators 1.856.277
Spectators per game (average) 35.698
Matches played 52
Scorers 99
Goals scored 146
Goal to match 2,8
Penalties 8
Players participating 390
Players sent off 5
The youngest Norman Whiteside (Northern Ireland) 17 years 41 days
Veteran Dino Zoff (Italy) 40 years 133 days
Top scorer Paolo Rossi (Italy) with 6 goals

POSTER

LOGO

ESPAÑA 82

MASCOTTE

FIFA World Cup

1986 in Mexico
Winner: ARGENTINA

FIRST STAGE IN GROUPS

GROUP A
ITALY - BULGARIA 1-1
ARGENTINA - SOUTH KOREA 3-1
ITALY - ARGENTINA 1-1
BULGARIA - SOUTH KOREA 1-1
ITALY - SOUTH KOREA 3-2
ARGENTINA 2-0 BULGARIA
Qualified: ARGENTINA - ITALY

GROUP B
MEXICO - BELGIUM 2-1
PARAGUAY - IRAQ 1-0
MEXICO - PARAGUAY 1-1
BELGIUM - IRAQ 2-1
MEXICO - IRAQ 1-0
BELGIUM - PARAGUAY 2-2
Qualified: MEXICO - PARAGUAY - BELGIUM

GROUP C
FRANCE - CANADA 1-0
USSR - HUNGARY 6-0
FRANCE - USSR 1-1
HUNGARY - CANADA 2-0
USSR - CANADA 2-0
FRANCE - HUNGARY 3-0
Qualified: USSR - FRANCE

GROUP D
BRAZIL - SPAIN 1-0
ALGERIA - NORTHERN IRELAND 1-1
BRAZIL - ALGERIA 1-0
SPAIN - NORTHERN IRELAND 2-1
BRAZIL - NORTHERN IRELAND 3-0
SPAIN - ALGERIA 3-0
Qualified: BRAZIL - SPAIN

GROUP E
DENMARK - SCOTLAND 1-0
W. GERMANY - URUGUAY 1-1
W. GERMANY - SCOTLAND 2-1
DENMARK - URUGUAY 6-1
SCOTLAND - URUGUAY 0-0
DENMARK - GERMANY O. 2-0
Qualified: DENMARK - WEST GERMANY - URUGUAY

GROUP F
POLAND - MOROCCO 0-'0
PORTUGAL - **ENGLAND** 1-0
ENGLAND - MOROCCO 0-0
POLAND - PORTUGAL 1-0
MOROCCO - PORTUGAL 3-1
ENGLAND - POLAND 3-0
Qualified:
MOROCCO - **ENGLAND** - POLAND

ROUND OF 16
MEXICO - BULGARIA 2-0
BELGIUM - USSR 4-3 a.d.
ARGENTINA - URUGUAY 1-0
BRAZIL - POLAND 4-0
FRANCE - ITALY 2-0
WEST GERMANY - MOROCCO 1-0
SPAIN - DENMARK 5-1
ENGLAND - PARAGUAY 3-0

ROUND OF 8
GERMANY W - MEXICO 4-1 pen.
FRANCE - BRAZIL 5-4 pen.
ARGENTINA - **ENGLAND** 2-1
BELGIUM - SPAIN 5-4 pen.

SEMIFINALS
GERMANY W - FRANCE 2-0
ARGENTINA - BELGIUM 2-0

FINAL 3rd PLACE
FRANCE - BELGIUM 4-2 et

FINAL
ARGENTINA - WEST GERMANY 3-2
22' Brown (ARG), 55' Valdano (ARG), 74' Rummenigge (FRG), 82' Völler (FRG), 88' Burruchaga (ARG)

FINAL RANKING
1° **ARGENTINA** 2° W. Germany 3° France 4° Belgium

WORLD CUP DATA

Edition XIII
Period from 31 May to 29 June 1986
Organizing country Mexico
Host cities Guadalajara, Irapuato, Leòn, Mexico City, Monterrey, Nezahualcòyotl, Puebla, Querétaro and Toluca
Final standings Argentina 1, West Germany 2, France 3, Belgium 4
Teams participating 24
Total spectators 2.407.431
Spectators per game (average) 46.297
Matches played 52
Scorers 79
Goals scored 132
Goals per game 2,53
Penalties 11
Players participating 414
Players sent off 8
The youngest Javier Cruz (Mexico) 20 years and 10 days
Veteran Patrick Jennings (Northern Ireland) 41 years old
Top scorer Gary Lineker (England) with 6 goals

POSTER

LOGO

MASCOTTE

FIFA World Cup

1990 in Italia
Winner: GERMANY

GROUP A
ITALY - AUSTRIA 1-0
CZECHOSLOVAKIA - USA 5-1
ITALY - USA 1-0
CZECHOSLOVAKIA - AUSTRIA 1-0
ITALY - CZECHOSLOVAKIA 2-0
AUSTRIA - USA 2-1
Qualified: ITALY - CZECHOSLOVAKIA

GROUP B
ROMANIA - USSR 2-0
CAMEROON - ARGENTINA 1-0
ARGENTINA - USSR 2-0
CAMEROON - ROMANIA 2-1
ARGENTINA - ROMANIA 1-1
USSR - CAMEROON 4-0
Qualified: CAMEROON - ROMANIA - ARGENTINA

GROUP C
BRAZIL - SWEDEN 2-1
COSTA RICA - SCOTLAND 1-0
SCOTLAND - SWEDEN 2-1
BRAZIL - COSTA RICA 1-0
BRAZIL - SCOTLAND 1-0
COSTA RICA - SWEDEN 2-1
Qualified: BRAZIL - COSTA RICA

GROUP D
ARAB EMIRATES - COLOMBIA 0-2
GERMANY - YUGOSLAVIA 4-1
YUGOSLAVIA - COLOMBIA 1-0
GERMANY - ARAB EMIRATES 5-1
YUGOSLAVIA - ARAB EMIRATES 4-1
GERMANY - COLOMBIA 1-1
Qualified: GERMANY - YUGOSLAVIA - COLOMBIA

GROUP E

BELGIUM - SOUTH KOREA 2-0
URUGUAY - SPAIN 0-0
SPAIN - SOUTH KOREA 3-1
BELGIUM - URUGUAY 3-1
URUGUAY - SOUTH KOREA 1-0
SPAIN 2-1 BELGIUM
Qualified: SPAIN - BELGIUM - URUGUAY

ROUND OF 16

CZECHOSLOVAKIA - COSTARICA 4-1
CAMEROON - COLOMBIA 2-1 et
BRAZIL - ARGENTINA 0-1
GERMANY 2-1 NETHERLANDS
ITALY - URUGUAY 2-0
IRELAND - ROMANIA 5-4 pen
ENGLAND - BELGIUM 1-0 et
YUGOSLAVIA - SPAIN 2-1 et

GROUP F

ENGLAND - IRELAND 1-1
HOLLAND - EGYPT 1-1
ENGLAND - NETHERLANDS 0-0
IRELAND - EGYPT 0-0
ENGLAND - EGYPT 1-0
HOLLAND - IRELAND 1-1
Qualified: **ENGLAND** - HOLLAND - IRELAND

ROUND OF 8

ITALY - IRELAND 1-0
ARGENTINA - YUGOSLAVIA 3-2 pen.
ENGLAND - CAMEROON 3-2 et
GERMANY - CZECHOSLOVAKIA 1-0

SEMIFINALS

ITALY - ARGENTINA 4-5 pen
GERMANY - **ENGLAND** 5-4 et

FINAL 3° PLACE
ITALY - ENGLAND 2-1
72' Baggio (ITA), 82' Platt (ENG), 86' rig. Schillaci (ITA)

FINAL
08/07/1990
GERMANY - ARGENTINA 1-0
84' Brehme (Pen.)

FINAL RANKING
1° GERMANY 2nd Argentina 3rd Italy 4th England

WORLD CUP DATA

Edition XIV
Period from 31 May to 29 June 1990
Organizing country Italy
Host cities Bari, Bologna, Cagliari, Florence, Genoa, Milan, Naples, Palermo, Rome, Turin, Udine and Verona
Final ranking West Germany 1, Argentina 2, Italy 3, England 4
Total spectators 2.517.348
Spectators per game (average) 48.411
Matches played 52
Scorers 74
Goals scored 115
Goals per game 2,21
Penalties 13
Players participating 412
Players sent off 16
The youngest Ronaldo Gonzales (Costa Rica) 19 years 307 days
Veteran Peter Shilton (England) 40 years and 298 days
Top scorer Salvatore Schillaci (Italy) with 6 goals

POSTER

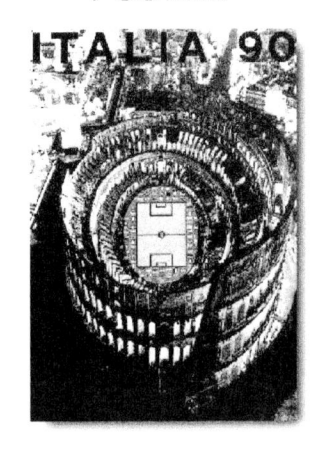

LOGO

MASCOTTE

FIFA World Cup

1994 negli U.S.A.
Winner: **BRASIL**

GROUP A
UNITED STATES - SWITZERLAND 1-1
COLOMBIA - ROMANIA 1-3
UNITED STATES - COLOMBIA 2-1
ROMANIA - SWITZERLAND 1-4
SWITZERLAND - COLOMBIA 0-2
UNITED STATES - ROMANIA 0-1
Qualified: ROMANIA - SWITZERLAND - UNITED STATES

GROUP B
SWEDEN 2-2 CAMEROON
BRAZIL - RUSSIA 2-0
BRAZIL - CAMEROON 3-0
SWEDEN - RUSSIA 3-1
RUSSIA - CAMEROON 6-1
BRAZIL - SWEDEN 1-1
Qualified: BRAZIL - SWEDEN

GROUP C
SPAIN - SOUTH KOREA 2-2
GERMANY - BOLIVIA 1-0
GERMANY - SPAIN 1-1
SOUTH KOREA - BOLIVIA 0-0
GERMANY - SOUTH KOREA 3-2
BOLIVIA - SPAIN 1-3
Qualified: GERMANY - SPAIN

GROUP D
NIGERIA 3-0 BULGARIA
ARGENTINA - GREECE 4-0
ARGENTINA - NIGERIA 2-1
BULGARIA - GREECE 4-0
NIGERIA - GREECE 2-0
BULGARIA - ARGENTINA 2-0
Qualified: NIGERIA - BULGARIA - ARGENTINA

GROUP E
ITALY - IRELAND 0-1
NORWAY - MEXICO 1-0
ITALY - NORWAY 1-0
MEXICO - IRELAND 2-1
ITALY - MEXICO 1-1
Qualified: MEXICO - IRELAND - ITALY

ROUND OF 16
SPAIN - SWITZERLAND 3-0
GERMANY - BELGIUM 3-2
ROMANIA - ARGENTINA 3-2
SAUDI ARABIA - SWEDEN 1-3
HOLLAND - IRELAND 2-0
BRAZIL - UNITED STATES 1-0
ITALY - NIGERIA 2-1 et
BULGARIA - MEXICO 4-2 pen

GROUP F
BELGIUM - MOROCCO 1-0
HOLLAND - SAUDI ARABIA 2-1
SAUDI ARABIA - MOROCCO 2-1
BELGIUM - NETHERLANDS 1-0
HOLLAND - MOROCCO 2-1
SAUDI ARABIA - BELGIUM 1-0
Qualified: HOLLAND - SAUDI ARABIA - BELGIUM

ROUND OF 8
ITALY - SPAIN 2-1
BRAZIL - SWEDEN 3-2
URUGUAY - GHANA 7-6 pen.
BULGARIA - GERMANY 2-1

SEMIFINALS
ITALY - BULGARIA 2-1
BRAZIL - SWEDEN 1-0

FINAL 3° PLACE
SWEDEN - BULGARIA 4-0

FINAL 17/07/1994 - Referee: Puhl (Hungary)
Rose Bowl - Los Angeles - Attendance: 94,000

BRAZIL - ITALY 3-2 pen.

Brazil: Taffarel; Jorginho, Aldair, M. Santos, Branco, Mazinho, Dunga, M. Silva, Zinho, Romario, Bebeto - Coach: Parreira

Italy: Pagliuca; Mussi, Maldini, Baresi, Benevento, Berti, Albertini, D. Baggio, Donadoni; R. Baggio, Massaro
Coach: Sacchi

FINAL RANKING
1° **BRASILE**   2° Italia   3° Svezia   4° Bulgaria

WORLD CUP DATA

Edition XV
Period from 17 June to 17 July 1994
Organizer country United States of America
Host Cities Boston, Chicago, Dallas, Detroit, New York, Orlando, Pasadena, San Francisco and Washington
Final ranking Brazil 1, Italy 2, Sweden 3, Bulgaria 4
Total spectators 3.587.538
Spectators per game (average) 68.991
Matches played 52
Scorers 79
Goals scored 147
Goals per game 2,82
Penalties 15
Players participating 428
Players sent off 15
The youngest Rigobert Song (Cameroon) 17 years and 353 days
Veteran Roger Milla (Cameroon) 42 years 39 days

LOGO

MASCOTTE

FIFA World Cup
1998 in France
Winner: **FRANCE**

GROUP A
MOROCCO - NORWAY 2-2
BRAZIL 2-1 SCOTLAND
SCOTLAND - NORWAY 1-1
BRAZIL - MOROCCO 3-0
SCOTLAND - MOROCCO 0-3
BRAZIL - NORWAY 1-2
Qualified: BRAZIL - NORWAY

GROUP B
CAMEROON - AUSTRIA 1-1
ITALY - CHILE 2-2
ITALY - CAMEROON 3-0
CHILE - AUSTRIA 0-1
ITALY - AUSTRIA 2-1
CHILE - CAMEROON 1-1
Qualified: ITALY - CHILE

GROUP C
FRANCE - SOUTH AFRICA 3-0
SAUDI ARABIA - DENMARK 0-1
SOUTH AFRICA - DENMARK 1-1
FRANCE - SAUDI ARABIA 4-0
FRANCE - DENMARK 2-1
SOUTH AFRICA - SAUDI ARABIA 2-2
Qualified: FRANCE DENMARK

GROUP D
PARAGAY - BULGARIA 0-0
SPAIN - NIGERIA 2-3
SPAIN - PARAGAY 0-0
NIGERIA - BULGARIA 1-0
SPAIN - BULGARIA 6-1
NIGERIA - PARAGAY 1-3
Qualified: NIGERIA - PARAGUAY

GROUP E
HOLLAND - BELGIUM 0-0
SOUTH KOREA - MEXICO 1-3
NETHERLANDS - SOUTH KOREA 5-0
BELGIUM - MEXICO 2-2
HOLLAND - MEXICO 2-2
BELGIUM - SOUTH KOREA 1-1
Qualified: NETHERLANDS - MEXICO

GROUP F
YUGOSLAVIA - IRAN 0-1
GERMANY - UNITED STATES 2-0
UNITED STATES - IRAN 1-2
GERMANY - YUGOSLAVIA 2-2
YUGOSLAVIA - UNITED STATES 1-0
GERMANY - IRAN 2-0
Qualified: GERMANY - YUGOSLAVIA

ROUND OF 16
ITALY - NORWAY 1-0
BRAZIL - CHILE 4-1
FRANCE - PARAGUAY 1-0 e.t.
NIGERIA - DENMARK 1-4
GERMANY - MEXICO 2-1
HOLLAND - YUGOSLAVIA 2-1
ROMANIA - CROATIA 0-1
ARGENTINA - ENGLAND 6-5 pen

GROUP G
ROMANIA - COLOMBIA 1-0
ENGLAND - TUNISIA 2-0
COLOMBIA 1-0 TUNISIA
ROMANIA - ENGLAND 2-1
ROMANIA - TUNISIA 1-1
COLOMBIA - ENGLAND 0-2
Qualified: ROMANIA - ENGLAND

GROUP H
ARGENTINA - JAPAN 1-2
JAMAICA - CROATIA 1-3
JAPAN 0-1 CROATIA
ARGENTINA - JAMAICA 5-0
JAPAN - JAMAICA 1-2
ARGENTINA - CROATIA 1-0
Qualified: ARGENTINA - CROATIA

ROUND OF 8
FRANCE - ITALY 0-0 (4-3 pen)
BRAZIL - DENMARK 3-2
ARGENTINA - NETHERLANDS 1-2
GERMANY - CROATIA 0-3

SEMIFINALS
BRAZIL - HOLLAND 1-1 (5-3 pen)
FRANCE - CROATIA 2-1

FINAL 3rd PLACE
HOLLAND - CROATIA 1-2

FINAL 12/07/1998
BRAZIL - FRANCE 0-3
27' e 45' Zidane, 90' Petit

FINAL RANKING
1° FRANCE   2° Brazil   3° Croatia   4° Holland

WORLD CUP DATA

Edition XVI
Period from 10 June to 12 July 1998
Organising country France
Host cities Bordeaux, Lens, Lyon, Marseille, Montpellier, Nantes, Paris, Saint Denis, Saint-Étienne, Toulouse
Final ranking France 1, Brazil 2, Croatia 3, Netherlands 4
Total spectators 2.785.100
Spectators per game (average) 43.517
Matches played 64
Scorers 107
Goals scored 171
Goals per game 2,67
Penalties 17
Players participating 573
Players sent off 22
The youngest Samuel Eto'o (Cameroon) 17 years 99 days
Veteran James Leighton (Scotland) 39 years and 300 days

LOGO

FRANCE 98
COUPE DU MONDE

POSTER

MASCOTTE

FIFA World Cup
2002 in South Corea/Japan
Winner: **BRASIL**

GROUP A
FRANCE - SENEGAL 0-1
URUGUAY - DENMARK 1-2
FRANCE - URUGUAY 0-0
DENMARK - SENEGAL 1-1
DENMARK - FRANCE 2-0
SENEGAL - URUGUAY 3-3
Qualified: DENMARK - SENEGAL

GROUP B
PARAGUAY - S. AFRICA 2-2
SPAIN - SLOVENIA 2-2
SPAIN - PARAGUAY 3-1
SOUTH AFRICA - SLOVENIA 1-0
SOUTH AFRICA - SPAIN 2-3
SLOVENIA - PARAGUAY 1-3
Qualified: SPAIN - PARAGUAY

GROUP C
BRAZIL 2-1 TURKEY
CHINA - COSTA RICA 0-1
BRAZIL - CHINA 4-0
COSTA RICA - TURKEY 1-1
COSTA RICA - BRAZIL 2-5
TURKEY - CHINA 3-0
Qualified: BRAZIL - TURKEY

GROUP D
SOUTH KOREA - POLAND 2-0
UNITED STATES - PORTUGAL 3-2
SOUTH KOREA - UNITED STATES 1-1
PORTUGAL - POLAND 4-0
PORTUGAL - SOUTH KOREA 0-1
POLAND - UNITED STATES 3-1
Qualified: SOUTH KOREA - UNITED STATES

FIFA World Cup

GROUP E
IRELAND - CAMEROON 1-1
GERMANY - ARABIA 8-0
GERMANY - IRELAND 1-1
CAMEROON - ARABIA 1-0
CAMEROON - GERMANY 0-2
ARABIA - IRELAND 0-3
Qualified: GERMANY - IRELAND

GROUP F
ENGLAND - SWEDEN 1-1
ARGENTINA- NIGERIA 1-0
SWEDEN - NIGERIA 2-1
ARGENTINA - ENGLAND 0-1
SWEDEN - ARGENTINA 1-1
NIGERIA - ENGLAND 0-0
Qualified: SWEDEN - ENGLAND

GROUP G
CROATIA - MEXICO 1-0
ITALY - ECUADOR 2-0
ITALY - CROATIA 1-2
MEXICO - ECUADOR 2-1
MEXICO - ITALY 1-1
ECUADOR - CROATIA 1-0
Qualified: MEXICO - ITALY

GROUP H
JAPAN - BELGIUM 2-2
RUSSIA - TUNISIA 2-0
JAPAN - RUSSIA 1-0
TUNISIA - BELGIUM 1-1
TUNISIA - JAPAN 0-2
BELGIUM - RUSSIA 3-2
Qualified: JAPAN - BELGIUM

ROUND OF 16
GERMANY - PARAGUAY 1-0
DENMARK - ENGLAND 0-3
SWEDEN - SENEGAL 1-2 e.t.
SPAIN - IRELAND 4-3 pen.
UNITED STATES - MEXICO 2-0
BRAZIL - BELGIUM 2-0
JAPAN - TURKEY 0-1
SOUTH KOREA - ITALY 2-1 (GOLDEN GOL)

ROUND OF 8
ENGLAND - BRAZIL 3-2
GERMANY - UNITED STATES 1-0
SPAIN - SOUTH KOREA 3-5 pen.
SENEGAL - TURKEY 0-1 e.t.

SEMIFINALS
GERMANY - SOUTH KOREA 1-0
BRAZIL - TURKEY 1-0

FINAL 3rd PLACE
SOUTH KOREA - TURKEY 2-3

FINAL 30/06/2002
GERMANY - BRAZIL 0-2
67 ' e 79' Ronaldo

FINAL RANKING
1° BRAZIL 2° Germany 3° Turkey 4° South Korea

WORLD CUP DATA

Edition XVII
Period from 31 May to 30 June 2002
Host countries South Korea and Japan
Host cities South Korea: Chongju, Inch'on, Kwangju, Pusan, Seogwipo, Seoul, Suwon, Taegu, Taejon, Ulsan;
Japan: Ibaraki, Kobe, Niigata, Oita, Osaka, Saitama, Sapporo, Sendai, Shizuoka, Yokohama
Final Ranking Brazil 1, Germany 2, Turkey 3, South Korea 4
Spectators per game 42268
Top scorer Ronaldo (Brazil) 8 goals
Matches played 64
Goals scored 161

LOGO

MASCOTTE

FIFA World Cup

2006 in Germany
Winner: ITALIA

GROUP A
GERMANY - COSTA RICA 4-2
POLAND - ECUADOR 0-2
GERMANY - POLAND 1-0
ECUADOR - COSTA RICA 3-0
ECUADOR - GERMANY 0-3
COSTA RICA - POLAND 1-2
Qualified: GERMANY - ECUADOR

GROUP B
ENGLAND - PARAGUAY 1-0
TRINIDAD AND TOBAGO - SWEDEN 0-0
ENGLAND - TRINIDAD AND TOBAGO 2-0
SWEDEN - PARAGUAY 1-0
SWEDEN - ENGLAND 2-2
PARAGUAY - TRINIDAD 2-0
Qualified: ENGLAND - SWEDEN

GROUP C
ARGENTINA - IVORY COAST 2-1
SERBIA AND MONTENEGRO - NETHERLANDS 0-1
ARGENTINA - SERBIA 4-0
NETHERLANDS - IVORY COAST 2-1
IVORY COAST - SERBIA 2-5
HOLLAND - ARGENTINA 0-0
Qualified: ARGENTINA - NETHERLANDS

GROUP D
MEXICO - IRAN 3-1
ANGOLA - PORTUGAL 0-1
MEXICO - ANGOLA 0-0
PORTUGAL - IRAN 2-0
IRAN - ANGOLA 1-1
PORTUGAL - MEXICO 2-1
Qualified: PORTUGAL - MEXICO

FIFA World Cup

GROUP E
UNITED STATES - CZECH REPUBLIC 0-3
ITALY - GHANA 2-0
ITALY - UNITED STATES 1-1
CZECH REPUBLIC - GHANA 0-2
GHANA - UNITED STATES 2-1
CZECH REPUBLIC - ITALY 0-2
Qualified: ITALY - GHANA

GROUP F
AUSTRALIA - JAPAN 3-1
BRAZIL - CROATIA 1-0
BRAZIL - AUSTRALIA 2-0
JAPAN 0-0 CROATIA
CROATIA - AUSTRALIA 2-2
JAPAN - BRAZIL 1-4
Qualified: BRAZIL - AUSTRALIA

ROUND OF 16
GERMANY - SWEDEN 2-0
ARGENTINA - MEXICO 2-1 e.t.
ENGLAND - ECUADOR 1-0
PORTUGAL 1-0 NETHERLANDS
ITALY - AUSTRALIA 1-0
SWITZERLAND - UKRAINE 0-3 pen.
BRAZIL - GHANA 3-0
SPAIN - FRANCE 1-3

GROUP G
FRANCE - SWITZERLAND 0-0
SOUTH KOREA - TOGO 2-1
FRANCE - SOUTH KOREA 1-2
TOGO - SWITZERLAND 0-2
SWITZERLAND - SOUTH KOREA 2-0
TOGO - FRANCE 0-2
Qualified: SWITZERLAND - FRANCE

GROUP H
SPAIN - UKRAINE 4-0
TUNISIA - SAUDI ARABIA 2-2
SPAIN - TUNISIA 3-1
SAUDI ARABIA - UKRAINE 0-4
UKRAINE - TUNISIA 1-0
SAUDI ARABIA - SPAIN 0-1
Qualified: SPAIN - UKRAINE

ROUND OF 8
GERMANY - ARGENTINA 5-3 pen.
ITALY - UKRAINE 3-0
ENGLAND - PORTUGAL 1-3 pen.
SENEGAL - FRANCE 0-1

SEMIFINALS
GERMANY - ITALY 0-2 e.t.
PORTUGAL - FRANCE 0-1

FINAL 3rd PLACE
GERMANY - PORTUGAL 3-1

FINAL - Olympic Stadium - Berlin - Spectators: 70,000 - Referee: Elizondo

ITALY - FRANCE 5-3 pen. (1-1)

7 'rig. Zidane (FRA), 19 'Materazzi (ITA)

ITALY: Buffon, Zambrotta, Cannavaro, Materazzi, Grosso, Gattuso, Pirlo, Camoranesi, Totti, Perrotta, Toni - Coach: Lippi

FRANCE: Barthez, Sagnol, Thuram, Gallas, Abidal, Makelele, Vieira, Ribery, Zidane, Malouda, Henry - Coach: Domenech

FINAL RANKING
1° ITALY   2° France   3° Germany   4° Portugal

WORLD CUP DATA

Edition XVIII
Period from 9 June to 9 July 2006
Organising country Germany
Host cities Kaiserslautern, Nuremberg, Hamburg, Berlin, Cologne, Dortmund, Frankfurt, Gelsenkirchen, Hanover, Munich and Stuttgart
Final ranking 1 Italy, 2 France, 3 Germany, 4 Portugal
Top scorer Miroslav Klose (Germany) 5
World Champions Players
1 Buffon Gianluigi (Juventus)
2 Zaccardo Cristian (Palermo)
3 Grosso Fabio (Palermo)
4 De Rossi Daniele (Roma)
5 Cannavaro Fabio (Juventus)
6 Barzagli Andrea (Palermo)
7 Del Piero Alessandro (Juventus)
8 Gattuso Gennaro Ivan (Milan)
9 Toni Luca (Fiorentina)
10 Totti Francesco (Roma)
11 Gilardino Alberto (Milan)
12 Peruzzi Angelo (Lazio)
13 Nesta Alessandro (Milan)
14 Amelia Marco (Livorno)
15 Iaquinta Vincenzo (Udinese)
16 Camoranesi Serra Mauro German (Juventus)
17 Barone Simone (Palermo)
18 Inzaghi Filippo (Milan)
19 Zambrotta Gianluca (Juventus)
20 Perrotta Simone (Roma)
21 Pirlo Andrea (Milan)
22 Oddo Massimo (Lazio)
23 Materazzi Marco (Inter)

LOGO

MASCOTTE

FIFA World Cup

2010 in Sudafrica
Winner: **SPAIN**

GROUP A
SOUTH AFRICA - MEXICO 1-1
URUGUAY - FRANCE 0-0
SOUTH AFRICA - URUGUAY 0-3
FRANCE - MEXICO 0-2
MEXICO - URUGUAY 0-1
FRANCE - SOUTH AFRICA 1-2
Qualified: URUGUAY - MEXICO

GROUP B
ARGENTINA - NIGERIA 1-0
SOUTH KOREA - GREECE 2-0
ARGENTINA - SOUTH KOREA 2-1
GREECE - NIGERIA 2-1
NIGERIA - SOUTH KOREA 2-2
GREECE - ARGENTINA 0-2
Qualified: ARGENTINA - SOUTH KOREA

GROUP C
ENGLAND - UNITED STATES 1-1
ALGERIA - SLOVENIA 0-1
SLOVENIA - UNITED STATES 2-2
ENGLAND - ALGERIA 0-0
SLOVENIA - ENGLAND 0-1
UNITED STATES - ALGERIA 1-0
Qualified: UNITED STATES - ENGLAND

GROUP D
SERBIA - GHANA 0-1
GERMANY - AUSTRALIA 4-0
GERMANY - SERBIA 0-1
GHANA - AUSTRALIA 1-1
GHANA - GERMANY 0-1
AUSTRALIA - SERBIA 2-1
Qualified: GERMANY - GHANA

GROUP E
HOLLAND - DENMARK 2-0
JAPAN -CAMEROON 1-0
HOLLAND - JAPAN 1-0
CAMEROON - DENMARK 1-2
DENMARK - JAPAN 1-3
CAMEROON - NETHERLANDS 1-2
Qualified: NETHERLANDS - JAPAN

GROUP F
ITALY - PARAGUAY 1-1
N. ZEALAND - SLOVAKIA 1-1
SLOVAKIA - PARAGUAY 0-2
ITALY - NEW ZEALAND 1-1
PARAGUAY-N.ZEALAND 0-0
SLOVAKIA - ITALY 3-2
Qualified: PARAGUAY - SLOVAKIA

GROUP G
IVORY COAST - PORTUGAL 0-0
BRAZIL - NORTH KOREA 2-1
BRAZIL - IVORY COAST 3-1
PORTUGAL - NORTH KOREA 7-0
PORTUGAL - BRAZIL 0-0
NORTH KOREA - IVORY COAST 0-3
Qualified: BRAZIL - PORTUGAL

GROUP H
HONDURAS - CHILE 0-1
SPAIN - SWITZERLAND 0-1
CHILE - SWITZERLAND 1-0
SPAIN - HONDURAS 2-0
CHILE - SPAIN 1-2
SWITZERLAND - HONDURAS 0-0
Qualified: SPAIN - CHILE

ROUND OF 16
URUGUAY - SOUTH KOREA 2-1
UNITED STATES - GHANA 1-2 e.t.
GERMANY - **ENGLAND** 4-1
ARGENTINA - MEXICO 3-1
HOLLAND - SLOVAKIA 2-1
BRAZIL - CHILE 3-0
PARAGUAY - JAPAN 5-3 pen.
SPAIN - PORTUGAL 1-0

ROUND OF 8
URUGUAY - GHANA 5-3 pen.
BRAZIL - NETHERLANDS 1-2
ARGENTINA - GERMANY 0-4
PARAGUAY - SPAIN 0-1

SEMIFINALS
URUGUAY - HOLLAND 2-3
GERMANY - SPAIN 0-1

FINAL 3rd PLACE
GERMANY - URUGUAY 3-1

FINAL 11/07/2010
HOLLAND - SPAIN 0-1 e.t.
116' Iniesta

FINAL RANKING
1° SPAIN   2° Holland   3° Germany   4° Uruguay

WORLD CUP DATA

Edition XIX
Period from 11 June to 11 July 2010
Organising country South Africa
Host cities Bloemfontein, Cape Town, Durban, Johannesburg (home to two facilities), Nelspruit, Polokwane, Port Elizabeth, Pretoria and Rustenburg
Final Ranking Spain 1, Holland 2, Germany 3 , Uruguay 4
Total audience 3.178.856
Spectators per game (average) 49.670
Matches played 64
Scorers 100
Own goals 2
Goals scored 149
Goals per game 2,328
Official song
As has been the case for some years now, even for South Africa 2010 a song is chosen as the anthem of the World Cup.
It is **Waka Waka** (This Time for Africa), played by the Colombian singer Shakira who years before had performed even before the final of the World Cup.

LOGO

MASCOTTE

FIFA World Cup
2014 in Brasil
Winner: GERMANY

GROUP A
BRAZIL - CROATIA 3-1
MEXICO - CAMEROON 1-0
BRAZIL - MEXICO 0-3
CAMEROON - CROATIA 4-0
CAMEROON - BRAZIL 1-4
CROATIA - MEXICO 1-3
Qualified: BRAZIL - MEXICO

GROUP B
HOLLAND - SPAIN 1-5
CHILE - AUSTRALIA 3-1
SPAIN - CHILE 0-2
AUSTRALIA - NETHERLANDS 2-3
AUSTRALIA - SPAIN 0-3
HOLLAND - CHILE 2-0
Qualified: NETHERLANDS - CHILE

GROUP C
COLOMBIA - GREECE 3-0
IVORY COAST - JAPAN 2-1
COLOMBIA - IVORY COAST 2-1
JAPAN - GREECE 0-0
JAPAN - COLOMBIA 1-4
GREECE - IVORY COAST 2-1
Qualified: COLOMBIA - GREECE

GROUP D
URUGUAY - COSTA RICA 1-3
ENGLAND - ITALY 1-2
URUGUAY - ENGLAND 2-1
ITALY - COSTA RICA 0-1
ITALY - URUGUAY 0-1
COSTA RICA - ENGLAND 0-0
Qualified: COSTA RICA - URUGUAY

GROUP E
SWITZERLAND - ECUADOR 2-1
FRANCE - HONDURAS 3-0
FRANCE - SWITZERLAND 5-2
HONDURAS - ECUADOR 1-2
HONDURAS - SWITZERLAND 0-3
ECUADOR - FRANCE 0-0
Qualified: FRANCE - SWISS

GROUP F
ARGENTINA 2-1 BOSNIA
IRAN - NIGERIA 0-0
ARGENTINA 1-0 IRAN
NIGERIA - BOSNIA 1-0
NIGERIA - ARGENTINA 2-3
BOSNIA - IRAN 3-1
Qualified: ARGENTINA NIGERIA

ROUND OF 16
BRAZIL - CHILE 4-3 pen.
COLOMBIA 2-0 URUGUAY
HOLLAND - MEXICO 2-1
COSTA RICA - GREECE 6-4 pen.
FRANCE 2-0 NIGERIA
GERMANY - ALGERIA 2-1 c.t.
ARGENTINA - SWITZERLAND 1-0 e.t.
BELGIUM - UNITED STATES 2-1 e.t.

GROUP G
GERMANY - PORTUGAL 4-0
GHANA - UNITED STATES 2-1
GERMANY - GHANA 2-2
UNITED STATES - PORTUGAL 2-2
UNITED STATES - GERMANY 0-1
PORTUGAL - GHANA 2-1
Qualified: GERMANY - UNITED STATES

GROUP H
BELGIUM - ALGERIA 2-1
RUSSIA - SOUTH KOREA 1-1
BELGIUM - RUSSIA 1-0
SOUTH KOREA - ALGERIA 2-4
SOUTH KOREA - BELGIUM 0-1
ALGERIA - RUSSIA 1-1
Qualified: BELGIUM - ALGERIA

ROUND OF 8
BRAZIL 2-1 COLOMBIA
FRANCE - GERMANY 0-1
HOLLAND - COSTA RICA 4-3 pen.
ARGENTINA - BELGIUM 1-0

SEMIFINALS
BRAZIL - GERMANY 1-7
HOLLAND - ARGENTINA 2-4 pen.

FINAL 3rd PLACE
BRAZIL - NETHERLANDS 0-3

FINAL 13 July 2014 - Maracanã Stadium - Rio de Janeiro
GERMANY - ARGENTINA 1-0 e.t.
113' Goetze

FINAL RANKING
1° GERMANY 2° Argentina 3° Brazil 4° Netherlands

WORLD CUP DATA

Edition XX (20)
Period from 12 June to 13 July 2014
Organizing country Brazil
Host cities Rio de Janeiro, Brasilia, São Paulo, Fortaleza, Salvador, Recife, Porto Alegre, Cuiaba, Natal, Curitiba and Manaus
Final ranking: Germany 1, Argentina 2, Holland 3, Brazil 4
Total spectators 3.429.873
Spectators per match (average) 53.592
Match played 64
Scorers 117
Own goals 5
Goals scored 171
Goals per game 2,67
The News: The spray can.
One of the the biggest news of the 2014 World Cup in Brazil is the introduction of spray cans for referees.
They'll be used to score the point of the ball and the barrier, so as to avoid the cunning ones who approach. It will become a standard everywhere later, but its introduction is in Brazil.

LOGO

FIFA WORLD CUP
Brasil

MASCOTTE

FIFA World Cup
2018 in Russia
Winner: **FRANCE**

GROUP A
RUSSIA - SAUDI ARABIA 5-0
EGYPT - URUGUAY 0-1
RUSSIA - EGYPT 3-1
URUGUAY - SAUDI ARABIA 1-0
URUGUAY - RUSSIA 3-0
SAUDI ARABIA - EGYPT 2-1
Qualified: URUGUAY - RUSSIA

GROUP B
MOROCCO - IRAN 0-1
PORTUGAL - SPAIN 3-3
PORTUGAL - MOROCCO 1-0
IRAN - SPAIN 0-1
IRAN - PORTUGAL 1-1
SPAIN - MOROCCO 2-2
Qualified: SPAIN - PORTUGAL

GROUP C
FRANCE - AUSTRALIA 2-1
PERU - DENMARK 0-1
DENMARK - AUSTRALIA 1-1
FRANCE - PERU 1-0
DENMARK - FRANCE 0-0
AUSTRALIA - PERU 0-2
Qualified: FRANCE - DENMARK

GROUP D
ARGENTINA - ICELAND 1-1
CROATIA - NIGERIA 2-0
ARGENTINA - CROATIA 3-0
NIGERIA - ICELAND 2-0
NIGERIA - ARGENTINA 1-2
ICELAND - CROATIA 1-2
Qualified: CROATIA - ARGENTINA

GROUP E
COSTA RICA - SERBIA 0-1
BRAZIL - SWITZERLAND 1-1
BRAZIL - COSTA RICA 2-0
SERBIA - SWITZERLAND 1-2
SERBIA - BRAZIL 0-2
SWITZERLAND - COSTA RICA 2-2
Qualified: BRAZIL - SWITZERLAND

GROUP F
GERMANY - MEXICO 0-1
SWEDEN - SOUTH KOREA 1-0
SOUTH KOREA - MEXICO 1-2
GERMANY - SWEDEN 2-1
SOUTH KOREA - GERMANY 2-0
MEXICO - SWEDEN 0-3
Qualified: SWEDEN - MEXICO

ROUND OF 16
URUGUAY - PORTUGAL 2-1
FRANCE - ARGENTINA 4-3
SPAIN - RUSSIA 4-5 pen
CROATIA - DENMARK 4-3 pen
BRAZIL - MEXICO 2-0
BELGIUM - JAPAN 3-2
SWEDEN - SWITZERLAND 1-0
COLOMBIA - **ENGLAND** 4-5 pen

GROUP G
BELGIUM - PANAMA 3-0
TUNISIA - **ENGLAND** 1-2
BELGIUM - TUNISIA 5-2
ENGLAND - PANAMA 6-1
ENGLAND - BELGIUM 0-1
PANAMA - TUNISIA 1-2
Qualified: BELGIUM - **ENGLAND**

GROUP H
COLOMBIA - JAPAN 1-2
POLAND - SENEGAL 1-2
JAPAN - SENEGAL 2-2
POLAND - COLOMBIA 0-3
JAPAN - POLAND 0-1
SENEGAL - COLOMBIA 0-1
Qualified: COLOMBIA - JAPAN

ROUND OF 8
URUGUAY - FRANCE 0-2
BRAZIL - BELGIUM 1-2
SWEDEN - **ENGLAND** 0-2
RUSSIA - CROATIA 5-6 pen
SEMIFINALS
FRANCE - BELGIUM 1-0
CROATIA - **ENGLAND** 2-1 et
FINAL 3rd PLACE
BELGIUM - **ENGLAND** 2-0

FINAL - 15/07/2018
FRANCE - CROATIA 4-2
18' aut. Mandžukic (CRO), 28' Perišic (CRO), 38' rig. Griezmann (FRA), 59' Pogba (FRA), 65' Mbappé (FRA), 69' Mandžukic (CRO)

FINAL RANKING
1° **FRANCE** 2° Croatia 3° Belgium 4° England

WORLD CUP DATA

Edition XXI (21)
Period from 14 June to 15 July 2018
Organising country Russia
Host cities Moscow Luzhniki Stadium, Otkrytie Arena in Moscow, Zenit Arena in Saint Petersburg, Baltika Arena in Kaliningrad, Kazan Arena in Kazan, Futbolnyj stadion v Samare in Sumara, Mordovija Arena in Saransk, Rostov Arena in Rostov on Don, Fišt Olympic Stadium in Soèi, Central Stadium of Yekaterinburg, Volgograd Volgograd Arena and Nizhny Novgorod Stadium
Final ranking 1 France, 2 Croatia, 3 Belgium, 4 E.gland
Total spectators 3.031,768
Spectators per game (average) 47.371
Matches 64
Scorers 110
Own goals 12
Goals scored 169
Goals per game 2,64

LOGO

FIFA WORLD CUP
RUSSIA 2018

MASCOTTE

2022 in QATAR
Winner: _____

WORLD CUP DATA

Edition XXII (22)
Period from 21 November to 18 December 2022
Organising Country Qatar
Host Cities   Lusail Iconic Stadium di Lusail, Al-Shamal Stadium di Madinat ash Shamal, Al-Khor Stadium di Al Khor, Al Wakrah Stadium di Al Wakrah, Qatar University Stadium, Sports City Stadium di Doha, Umm Salal Stadium di Umm Salal, Doha Port Stadium di Doha, Education City Stadium, Ahmed bin Ali Stadium, Al Gharafa Stadium
Matches played 64
Goals scored:
Top Scorer:

LOGO

MASCOTTE

FINAL RANKING:
1° _____
2° _____
3° _____
4° _____

FIFA World Cup

General Statistics and Records

FIFA World Cup

FIFA World Cup

MATCHES AND RESULTS FINAL PHASE WORLD CUP
- RANKING BY COUNTRIES -

NAZIONE	PG	V	N	S	GF	GS
BRAZIL	109	73	18	18	229	105
GERMANY	109	67	20	22	226	125
ITALY	83	45	21	17	128	77
ARGENTINA	81	43	15	23	137	93
ENGLAND	69	29	21	19	91	64
FRANCE	66	34	13	19	120	77
SPAIN	63	30	15	18	99	72
MEXICO	57	16	14	27	60	98
URUGUAY	56	24	12	20	87	74
SWEDEN	51	19	13	19	80	73
HOLLAND	50	27	12	11	86	48
BELGIUM	48	20	9	19	68	71
RUSSIA	45	19	10	16	77	54
YUGOSLAVIA	37	16	8	13	60	46
SWISS	37	12	8	17	50	64
POLAND	34	16	5	13	46	45
SOUTH KOREA	34	6	9	19	34	70
CHILE	33	11	7	15	40	49
UNITED STATES	33	8	6	19	37	62
HUNGARY	32	15	3	14	87	57
CZECHOSLOVAKIA	30	11	5	14	44	45

FIFA World Cup

PORTUGAL	30	14	6	10	49	35
AUSTRIA	29	12	4	13	43	47
PARAGUAY	27	7	10	10	30	38
BULGARIA	26	3	8	15	22	53
CAMEROON	23	4	7	12	18	43
CROATIA	23	11	4	8	35	26
SCOTLAND	23	4	7	12	25	41
COLOMBIA	22	9	3	10	32	30
JAPAN	21	5	5	11	20	29
NIGERIA	21	6	3	12	23	30
ROMANIA	21	8	5	8	30	32
DENMARK	20	9	5	6	30	26
COSTA RICA	18	5	5	8	19	28
PERU'	18	5	3	10	21	33
SAUDI ARABIA	16	3	2	11	11	39
AUSTRALIA	16	2	4	10	13	31
MOROCCO	16	2	5	9	14	22
IRAN	15	2	4	9	9	24
TUNISIA	15	2	4	9	13	25
ALGERIA	13	3	3	7	13	19
EIRE	13	2	8	3	10	10
IRELAND	13	3	5	5	13	23

FIFA World Cup

GHANA	12	4	3	5	13	16
ECUADOR	10	4	1	5	10	11
GREECE	10	2	2	6	5	20
TURKEY	10	5	1	4	20	17
IVORY COAST	9	3	1	5	13	14
HONDURAS	9	0	3	6	3	14
SOUTH AFRICA	9	2	4	3	11	16
NORWAY	8	2	3	3	7	8
SENEGAL	8	3	3	2	11	10
NORTH KOREA	7	1	1	5	6	21
EGYPT	7	0	2	5	5	12
BOLIVIA	6	0	1	5	1	20
EL SALVADOR	6	0	0	6	1	22
EAST GERMANY	6	2	2	2	5	5
NEW ZELAND	6	0	3	3	4	14
SERBIA	6	2	0	4	4	7
SLOVENIA	6	1	1	4	5	10
WALES	5	1	3	1	4	4
UKRAINE	5	2	1	2	5	7
SLOVAKIA	4	1	1	2	5	7
ANGOLA	3	0	2	1	1	2
BOSNIA	3	1	0	2	4	3

FIFA World Cup

CANADA	3	0	0	3	0	5
CHINA	3	0	0	3	0	9
CUBA	3	1	1	1	5	12
ARAB EMIRATES	3	0	0	3	2	11
JAMAICA	3	1	0	2	3	9
HAITI	3	0	0	3	2	14
IRAQ	3	0	0	3	1	4
ICELAND	3	0	1	2	2	5
ISRAEL	3	0	2	1	1	3
KUWAIT	3	0	1	2	2	6
PANAMA	3	0	0	3	2	11
CZECH REPUBLIC	3	1	0	2	3	4
SERBIA AND MONTENEGRO	3	0	0	3	2	10
TOGO	3	0	0	3	1	6
TRINIDAD AND TOBAGO	3	0	1	2	0	4
ZAIRE	3	0	0	3	0	14
DUTCH INDIES	1	0	0	1	0	6

* GERMANY also includes "WEST GERMANY"

LEGENDA
PG = Games Played   V = Wins   N = Draws
S = Losses   GF = Goals scored   GS = Goals conceded

FIFA World Cup

- GENERAL RANKING WORLD PODIUMS -

NATION	WINNER	FINAL	SEMIFINAL
BRAZIL	5	7	11
GERMANY	4	8	13
ITALY	4	6	8
ARGENTINA	2	5	5
FRANCE	2	3	6
URUGUAY	2	2	5
ENGLAND	1	1	3
SPAIN	1	1	2
HOLLAND	0	3	5
HUNGARY	0	2	2
CZECHOSLOVAKIA	0	2	2
SWEDEN	0	1	4
YUGOSLAVIA	0	0	2
AUSTRIA	0	0	2
POLAND	0	0	2
PORTUGAL	0	0	2
RUSSIA	0	0	1
CHILE	0	0	1
BELGIUM	0	0	2
BULGARIA	0	0	1
CROATIA	0	1	2
USA	0	0	1
SOUTH COREA	0	0	1
TURKEY	0	0	1

INDIVIDUAL RECORDS

More convocations:
5 Antonio Carbajal - Mexico (1950-1954-1958-1962-1966)
5 Lothar Matthäus - Germany (1982-1986-1990-1994-1998)
5 Gianluigi Buffon - Italy (1998-2002-2006-2010-2014)
5 Rafael Márquez - Mexico (2002-2006-2010-2014-2018)
More games played
25 Lothar Matthäus - Germany (2 in 1982, 7 in 1986, 7 in 1990, 5 in 1994, 4 in 1998)[6]
24 Miroslav Klose - Germany (7 in 2002, 7 in 2006, 5 in 2010, 5 in 2014)
23 Paolo Maldini - Italy (7 in 1990, 7 in 1994, 5 in 1998, 4 in 2002)
Winners from player and coach. In parentheses the triumphs as coach,
Franz Beckenbauer - Germany 2 1974, (1990)
Didier Deschamps - France 2 1998, (2018)
DISCIPLINE
Greater number of expulsions
2 Rigobert Song - Cameroon (one in 1994 and the other in 1998)
2 Zinédine Zidane - France (one in 1998 and the other in 2006)
Greater number of cards.
6 Cafu - Brazil (6 yellow and 0 red)
6 Zinédine Zidane - France (4 yellow and 2 red)
GOAL
More goals scored
16 Miroslav Klose - Germany (5-2002, 5-2006, 4-2010, 2-2014)
Matches with at least 1 goal scored: 11 Ronaldo - Brazil
More goals scored in a single edition
13 nets: Just Fontaine - Sweden195
More editions ended with at least one goal
4 Pelé Brazil (6-1958,1-1962,1-1966,4-1970), Uwe Seeler West Germany (2 in 1958, 2 in 1962, 2 in 1966, 3 in 1970), Miroslav Klose Germany (5 in 2002, 5 in 2006, 4 in 2010, 2 in 2014), Cristiano Ronaldo Portugal (1 in 2006, 1 in 2010, 1 in 2014, 4 in 2018)
More goals in a match
5 Oleg Salenko - Russia (Russia-Cameroon 6-1, 1994, Group B)

Later goal
120 minutes and 51 seconds - Djabou - Algeria (2014, Germany-Algeria 2-1 dts)
Faster goals
11 seconds: Hakan Sükür - Turkey - South Korea 3 - 2 - Final 3rd/4th place Giapppone/korea 2002
15 seconds: Václav Mašek - Czechoslovakia - Mexico Stage in Gironi (3rd Group) 1 - 3 1962 Chile
23 seconds: Pak Seung-Zin - North Korea - Portugal Quarter-finals 3 - 5 1966 England
AGE
Younger player
Norman Whiteside (17 years, 41 days) - Yugoslavia - Northern Ireland 0-0, 1982, first round, Group E
Older player
Essam El-Hadary (45 years, 161 days) - Saudi Arabia - Egypt 2-1, 2018, first round, group A
Younger scorer
Pelé (17 years, 239 days) - Brazil - Wales 1-0, 1958, quarter-finals
Older scorer
Roger Milla (42 years, 39 days) - Cameroon-Russia 1-6, 1994, first round, group B
Youngest World Champion Ever:
Pelé - Brazil (17 years, 249 days) - in Sweden 29 June 1958
Oldest World Champion Ever:
Dino Zoff - Italy (40 years, 134 days) - Madrid (Spain), 11 July 1982
Greater unbeatability of a goalkeeper
518 minutes Walter Zenga - Italy (1990, from 1' of the first match to 68' of the semifinal);
Fewer goals conceded throughout the tournament
2 goals: Walter Zenga Italia 1990 - Fabien Barthez Francia 1998 - Gianluigi Buffon Italia 2006 - Iker Casillas Spagna 2010)
COACHES
Most matches: 25 Helmut Schön - West Germany (6 in 1966, 6 in 1970, 7 in 1974, 6 in 1978).
Most world titles: 2 Vittorio Pozzo - Italy (1934, 1938).

FIFA World Cup

TEAMS RECORDS

Average goals per match: 5,4 - Hungary (1954, in five matches)
Goals scored in a single edition: 27 Hungary (1954, in five games)
Goals conceded in a single edition: 16 South Korea (1954, 9 from Hungary and 7 from Turkey)
Scored in a single game: 10 Hungary (1982, Hungary-El Salvador 10-1, II Girone)
Goals conceded in a single game: 10 El Salvador (1982, Hungary-El Salvador 10-1, II Girone)
Fewer goals in one edition: 0 Switzerland (2006, 4 games), Switzerland went out in the eighth place against Ukraine losing 3-0 at the penalty shootout
Consecutive wins (single edition): 7 Brazil (2002, all games)
Consecutive victories (multiple editions): 11 Brazil (7 in 2002, 4 in 2006)
Consecutive games without victory: 17 Bulgaria (from debut in 1962 to 1994)
No-loss matches (consecutive editions): 13 Brazil (6 in 1958, 6 in 1962, 1 in 1966)
Unbeatable goalkeeper: 518 minutes Italy (1990)
Most games won at penalty shootouts: 4 Germany, Argentina
Most games lost in penalty shootouts: 3 Italy, England, Spain
Most games played: 109 Germany (including 1954 to 1990, when it played as West Germany) (in 19 appearances) and Brazil (in 21 appearances)
Most networks built: 229 Brazil
Most goals conceded: 125 Germany (including editions from 1954 to 1990, when he participated as West Germany)
Most wins: 73 Brazil

Most draws: 21 Italy, England
Most losses: 27 Mexico
Most participations: 21 Brazil (all issues)
Most finals played: 8 Germany
Most finals won: 5 Brazil (out of six played, in addition to the final round match of 1950)
Most finals lost: 4 Germany (out of eight played)
Most places in the top four: 13 Germany

MATCH RECORDS

Most played match: Brazil-Sweden, Germany-Yugoslavia (now Serbia) and Germany-Argentina, 7 times
Most played game in consecutive editions: Italy-Argentina, 5 times from 1974 to 1990.
Cards in a match: 16 (Portugal-Netherlands 2006, eighth in the final)
Red cards in a match: 4 (2006, Portugal-Netherlands, eighth in the final, 2 expulsions per side)
Goals in one match: 12 (1954, Switzerland-Austria 7-5, quarter-finals)
Goals in opening match: 6 (2006, Germany-Costa Rica 4-2)
Goals in a tied match: 8 (1954, England-Belgium 4-4 and 1962, USSR-Colombia 4-4)
Goals in overtime: 5 (1970, Italy-Germany 4-3, 1-1 in 90% balance)

FIFA World Cup

Notes

FIFA World Cup

Notes

Printed in Great Britain
by Amazon